2003
Ian—
Lessons from
Mom Love, Mom

As a Gentleman Would Say

AS A GENTLEMAN WOULD SAY

RESPONSES TO LIFE'S IMPORTANT (AND SOMETIMES AWKWARD) SITUATIONS

by

JOHN BRIDGES AND BRYAN CURTIS

Rutledge Hill Press®
Nashville, Tennessee

A Division of Thomas Nelson, Inc.
www.ThomasNelson.com

Published by Rutledge Hill Press, a Division of Thomas Nelson, Inc., P.O. Box 141000, Nashville, Tennessee 37214.

Library of Congress Cataloging-in-Publication Data

Bridges, John, 1950–
    As a gentleman would say : responses to life's important (and sometimes awkward) situations / by John Bridges and Bryan Curtis.
        p. cm.
    ISBN 1-55853-846-1
    1. Etiquette for men. 2. Conversation. I. Curtis, Bryan. II. Title.

BJ1601 .B75 2001
395.1'42—dc21

                                                    2001020488

Printed in the United States of America

3 4 5 6 7 8 9—05 04 03 02 01

CONTENTS

INTRODUCTION

The military can train a man to react without thinking when he is under enemy fire. A good accounting course can teach any businessman how to read a spreadsheet with absolute ease. A seasoned quarterback can know what play to call, almost instinctively, in the heat of even the closest game. But the sight of a would-be love interest, the prospect of a dinner party, or the presence of a bereaved coworker can reduce even the bravest hero to mumbling gibberish. Even though he has the best of intentions, a gentleman oftentimes finds himself fumbling for words. He means well, but for the life of him he can't think of what he means to say at the moment. When he should be taking a deep breath and composing his thoughts, he finds himself blurting out something he would never intentionally say.

Of course a gentleman knows what fork to use, he opens the door for others, and he always puts the toilet lid back down. But gentlemanliness goes deeper than mere nice manners, it requires preparation, so that, whenever possible, a gentleman can do his part to make the world a much nicer place in which to live. Because he knows that a thoughtless comment can forever diminish the way others view a person, a gentleman does not open his mouth without thinking ahead. Oftentimes a gentleman is put to the test when he is least expecting it. He is introduced to a new friend at a cocktail party, and he can think of nothing except the ungainliness of the new friend's hairpiece. A longtime acquaintance strides up, extends his hand, and the gentleman's mind goes blank. A coworker has just had a miscarriage, and the gentleman wants to say something, but he does not know, precisely, the right thing to say. These awkward moments, and others like them, come to a gentleman far too regularly over the course of his life.

If a gentleman is prepared, he can handle almost any awkward social situation. The basic rule is to say as little as possible, but to choose those few words with the utmost care. A gentleman knows that when he expresses his sympathy, he is not expected to heal the pain of parents who have lost a child in a horrible automobile accident. At the same time, he knows that even in lighter moments he is not perfect. If he forgets a name, he can admit the gaffe and be forgiven. He knows, too, that he must stand up for himself and whenever possible say what he thinks. If a friend asks him to lie, he declines to participate in the deception. If he is treated rudely in a restaurant, he knows how to lodge his complaint as well as how to determine the person with whom it should be lodged. If he has strong feelings about politics or religion, he knows when and where those opinions should be voiced. And despite whatever others may think, he knows that being a gentleman has nothing to do with being a doormat. It is not an inevitability, he knows, that good guys must always finish last. In matters of love and friendship, saying the right thing is of vital importance. But a real gentleman knows that sometimes, when words seem to have lost all usefulness, being silent can be the right thing too.

Knowing what to say, and more importantly what not to say, in life's important situations, is a priceless skill. The drill sergeant trains his soldiers to react without thinking under enemy fire; the professor teaches the potential businessman to read a spreadsheet; the coach prepares his quarterback to know what play to call. This book exists to prepare a gentleman for those moments when he, too, will have to spring to action. It provides the ammunition and the strategies he will need to survive even the most embarrassing encounters.

A gentleman knows that saying the right thing is not about being quick and clever. Instead he has higher priorities. A gentleman makes others feel better about themselves. He wants to put himself in the other person's place. He wants life to run more smoothly not just for himself, but for the people he counters in the normal course of life. He wants to be part of the solution to life's problems—especially the ones over which he has some small amount of control. At the very least, he does not add to the unavoidable awkwardness that is an all-too-common part of human existence. That, he knows, is what gentlemanliness is all about.

When a gentleman speaks, he hopes to sound wise, or—at the very least—he hopes to bring a smile to someones face. He never uses words to harm or demean another person. Even when he is silent, he can be eloquent, offering a listening ear, or a shoulder for a friend to lean upon.

53 THINGS EVERY WELL-SPOKEN GENTLEMAN KNOWS

A gentleman knows how to begin a conversation.

———

A gentleman always thinks before he speaks. He also thinks after he speaks, in order to build upon the rightness, or correct the wrongness, of what he might have said.

———

If a gentleman is subjected to a rude remark or rude behavior, he does not offer rudeness in return.

———

A gentleman allows others to finish their sentences. Even in his most brilliant moments, he does not interrupt others, no matter how dull their opinions might be.

———

A gentleman does not talk with his mouth full—even over the phone.

———

A gentleman is slow to judge the actions of others, either in their public or private affairs.

———

A gentleman does not take part in major arguments over minor issues.

———

When a gentleman learns that two friends are to be married, he tells the groom-to-be, "Congratulations," and says, "Best wishes" to the soon-to-be bride.

———

A gentleman makes a conscious effort to use correct grammar, but he resists all temptation to sound stuffy and overly grand.

———

Unless he is teaching an English class, a gentleman does not correct another person's grammar.

———

A gentleman does not use foreign phrases, unless he is absolutely sure of their meaning—and their pronunciation.

———

A gentleman does not pretend to speak languages that he has not made his own.

———

A gentleman is careful of what he says in the presence of people speaking foreign languages. They may understand what he is saying even though he might not understand them.

———

Even when speaking his own language, a gentleman does not use words that he can define only by looking them up in a dictionary.

———

Once a gentleman has learned a new word from the dictionary, he attempts to use it correctly, thereby making it his own.

———

A gentleman never asks a woman
if she is pregnant.

———

Even in the most heated discussion, a
gentleman avoids raising his voice. He
does not shout others down.

———

When a gentleman inconveniences
another person by asking him or her
to shift so that he can move through
a crowded room, he says, "Excuse me."
He does not say, "I'm sorry," since
there is no reason for him to
apologize. In fact, a gentleman
never says, "I'm sorry," unless he
has given offense.

———

A gentleman never begins a
statement with "I don't mean to
embarrass you but . . ."

———

A gentleman does not ask
anyone—male or female—to divulge
his or her age.

———

When a gentleman initiates
a telephone conversation,
he knows it is his responsibility
to end that conversation.

————

A gentleman does not use his
cell phone when he is at a table
with others.

————

Once a gentleman discovers that
he must decline an invitation that he has
already accepted, he promptly alerts
his host or hostess. He gives a frank
description of the reasons
for his change of plan and offers
a sincere apology.

————

When a gentleman receives a number
of invitations on his answering service,
he accepts the first one. Even in the
world of voice mail, it is rude to weigh
one invitation against another.

————

When it comes to accepting social
invitations, a gentleman never waits for
something better to come along.

————

A gentleman does not engage
in arguments, of any sort, at
the dinner table.

———

When a gentleman is confronted by
arguments that he considers foolish,
he does not attempt to refute them
with reason. Instead, he keeps silent,
knowing that logic is useless in the
war against irrationality.

———

A gentleman gives direct answers,
especially to controversial questions.
Being direct, however, is not the
same thing as being rude.

———

A gentleman never claims to have
seen a movie he has not seen or to
have read a book about which he has
only read reviews. He knows how to
say, "I haven't read (or seen) that yet,
but from what I hear about it, it sounds
very interesting. What do you think?"

———

In civil conversation, and when
attempting to meet new friends, a
gentleman asks the question, "What do
you think?" as often as possible.

———

A gentleman does not brag, especially about his own accomplishments.

———

A gentleman knows that the best kind of small talk consists of asking questions, not volunteering information about himself.

———

A gentleman never says, "I told you so."

———

A gentleman knows how to make an apology—and how to accept one.

———

A gentleman knows how to extend a compliment—and how to receive one.

———

A gentleman avoids left-handed compliments at all costs.

———

A gentleman knows how to make an introduction.

———

A gentleman knows how to shake hands and is ready to do so.

———

A gentleman does not spread rumors. He is even careful about where he spreads sensitive facts.

———

A gentleman always attempts to make sure his breath is fresh, especially if he expects to be in close conversation with others. If necessary, he carries—and uses—breath mints.

———

A gentleman makes an effort to keep his hands, especially his fingernails, clean at all times. He never knows when he will be introduced to a new acquaintance, and he never wants to be reluctant to extend his hand in greeting.

———

A gentleman always carries a clean handkerchief and is ready to offer it in times of great grief—or great joy.

———

Whenever a gentleman requests any service or favor, he remembers to say, "Please." He is quick to say, "Thank you," whenever a service or favor has been offered to him.

———

When he is invited to participate in some pleasant experience—whether it is a dinner party or major-league baseball game—a gentleman does not dally before saying yes.

———

A gentleman understands the meaning of the word *no*.

———

A gentleman knows how to listen.

———

A gentleman knows that listening is a skill that improves when it is regularly practiced.

———

When a gentleman feels that he has been subjected to an insult, he immediately knows the right response: He responds by saying nothing at all.

———

A gentleman has definite beliefs, but he thinks before voicing his opinions. He recognizes that other people's beliefs are valid. He argues only over an issue that could save a life.

———

In making after-work conversation, a gentleman is wise to leave his work at the office.

———

A gentleman does not openly attempt to correct the behavior of his friends. Instead he teaches by example.

———

A gentleman takes no part in petty arguments over important topics. Instead, he takes action to bring about change.

———

A gentleman knows how to end a conversation.

———

AROUND TOWN

When a gentleman encounters an acquaintance who greets him with "Hi. How are you?" . . .

He does not say:

"Actually, I'm having a lousy day. My car's in the shop, and I had to take the dog to the vet. What's worse, I'm behind on my house payment and my girlfriend left me."

"Just great. The promotion came through, and Rolfy just had puppies. Want to see the pictures?"

"What's it to you?"

But he does say:

"Fine. How about you?"

In casual discourse, there are few questions that do not require an answer. This is one of them. Even on his worst days, a gentleman does not stop traffic on the sidewalk so that he can share his woes with an acquaintance who merely intended to say something a little more expansive than a simple "Hello."

When a Gentleman Runs Into a Friend Who Has Obviously Had Cosmetic Surgery . . .

He does not say:

"Who did your work? I bet it cost a bundle."

"Personally, I plan to grow old gracefully."

"When are you going to have the rest of it done?"

"It's none of my business, but I thought you looked better before."

"If I were you, I'd get my nose done next."

But he does say:

"Hello, Catherine [or Calvin], you're looking great!"

Whether he approves or disapproves of cosmetic surgery, a gentleman has to admit that it creates a social dilemma. His friend has gone under the knife for the purpose of improving his or her appearance. Yet, if the surgery has been successful, its results should be so natural-looking that they are not worth mentioning. A gentleman is better off mentioning a general improvement in his friend's appearance, avoiding the specifics at all costs.

WHEN A GENTLEMAN ENCOUNTERS A FRIEND WHO HAS OBVIOUSLY PUT ON WEIGHT . . .

He does not say:

"Man, you're bursting out of that jacket, aren't you?"

"I know this great diet—if you want it."

"Why don't you meet me tomorrow morning at the gym? We need to get some of that fat off of you."

"Are you sure you need that second helping of cocktail weenies?"

But he does say:

"Tony, it's great to see you."

A gentleman knows that another person's weight gain, or loss, is absolutely none of his business. He also knows that his wisest course is to shore up a friend's self-esteem, rather than destroy the friend's self-image. Weight gain might be the result of an incapacitating illness, stress, or some other emotional problem. When the friend eventually asks the gentleman's advice, the gentleman may offer it freely, always remembering the other person's feelings. Until then, however, he keeps his opinions to himself.

WHEN A GENTLEMAN ENCOUNTERS
A FRIEND WHO HAS RECENTLY BEEN
DIAGNOSED WITH A SERIOUS,
PERHAPS INCURABLE, ILLNESS . . .

He does not say:
"What do you think caused it?"

"Did they tell you how much time you've got?"

"Do you have a will?"

"Bet you wish you'd taken better care of yourself."

"You're looking really good, all things considered."

But he does say:
"Hello, Jessica, how are you doing?"

When a gentleman asks this question, he is
not asking for a prognosis, and he allows his
friend to answer it in any way he or she prefers.
If the friend is able to attend a party, clearly he
or she would rather not discuss doctors and
hospitals. The gentleman follows the friend's
lead in the conversation and feels free to share
the news of his own life since that is very likely
what his friend would rather hear. At the end of
their encounter, the gentleman might, however,
want to add, "Let's keep in touch. I want to hear
how things are going."

WHEN A GENTLEMAN, AT A PARTY, RUNS
INTO A FRIEND WHO HAS OBVIOUSLY
HAD AN INJURY—PARTICULARLY AN
INJURY THAT HAS LEFT SCARS . . .

He does not say:
  "Did that hurt?"

  "I bet the other guy looks rough."

  "Are you always going to have that?"

  "Has Michael been beating you again?"

But he does say:
  Nothing, unless a comment is absolutely
  unavoidable.

If a friend is on crutches or if his face is
swathed in bandages, a gentleman would be less
than human if he did not ask, "Jim, what's
happened?" Still, he is discreet enough to allow
his friend to divulge as little, or as much,
information as he chooses. If it appears that the
injury has left his friend disfigured, a gentleman
does not comment on that fact, since it will
probably be part of his friend's life from then
on. At any rate, a gentleman never makes light
of another person's distress or discomfort.

When a gentleman runs into a friend who has been fired from his job . . .

He does not say:

"How long before you're in financial trouble?"

"What kind of severance package did you get?"

"Are you going to sue?"

"I wish I could get fired. I'd love to live on unemployment for a while."

But he does say:

"I hear you've left the bank. How are things going?"

A gentleman allows his friend to give the details of "leaving" his job. If the friend divulges the facts of his termination, a gentleman may respond by saying, "That sounds really, really tough," not encouraging him to rehash the painful saga. If the friend, however, chooses to discuss his job search, a gentleman is unfailingly encouraging, saying, "You're a bright guy, Malcolm. Once you're over this hurdle, the right door is going to open, I know." He does not, however, overburden his friend with advice about what *he* would do. No two people's careers ever follow precisely the same track.

WHEN A GENTLEMAN ENCOUNTERS A FRIEND WHO HAS OBVIOUSLY LOST A GREAT DEAL OF WEIGHT . . .

He does not say:
"Have you been sick?"

"Man, you must have lost fifty pounds. Don't you think it's time to stop?"

"I'm glad you've lost some weight. How do you plan to keep it off?"

"How much more do you want to lose?"

But he does say:
"You look fabulous. Is that a new dress (or a new sports coat)?"

It is not necessary to make specific mention of a friend's weight loss. When a gentleman compliments a friend's appearance, the friend will get the message and might likely be relieved to think the compliment is the result of a whole new sense of well-being, not just the loss of some extra pounds. If a gentleman has any suspicion at all that a friend's weight loss is the result of illness, he does not mention that possibility in public—neither does he spread such rumors among his acquaintances.

When a friend's team loses, and the gentleman's team is the winner . . .

He does not say:

"Guess that's the last time you'll be cheering for those losers."

"How 'bout those guys of mine? Aren't they great?"

"Did you see that last play? You guys didn't have a chance."

"I told you your guys can't play worth crap."

But he does say:

"Tough break, Harry. You guys played a great game."

A gentleman feels no need to apologize for his team's victory. On the other hand, he does not revel in his friend's loss. Since the gentleman was rooting for the winning team and is in a mood to celebrate, he may even offer to buy his friend a couple of beers.

WHEN A GENTLEMAN'S TEAM LOSES, AND HIS FRIEND'S TEAM IS THE WINNER . . .

He does not say:

"I can't believe the way you guys cheated."

"What's with those refs? Are they blind?"

"If we'd had last year's lineup, this would have been a different story."

But he does say:

"Congratulations. I have to admit it: You guys really played a great game."

A gentleman does not downplay the victors' triumph. Neither does he berate his own team's performance. He resists all temptation to be a sore loser, knowing that there will always be another ball game. If, however, he chooses not to be present for his friend's rejoicing, he may bow out on the post-game festivities.

FRIENDS AND LOVERS

WHEN A GENTLEMAN IS INVITED TO A WEDDING WHERE THE BRIDE IS A FORMER GIRLFRIEND . . .

He does not say:

"I guess she just wants to rub my face in it."

"If she's crazy enough to think I'm giving her a gift . . ."

"Just wait until I tell him what he's getting into."

"This must be her mother's idea."

But he does say:

"I'm happy for her and wish her all the best." He then gracefully accepts or declines the invitation.

A gentleman need not assume there is malevolent motivation behind an old flame's every action. If the sting of an old romance is still sharp, he may simply decline to participate in the happy nuptials. On the other hand, if he is willing to bury the hatchet, he sends a gift, dresses himself appropriately, and proceeds to have a good time at the party. After all, he knows that wedding receptions are a matchmaking paradise.

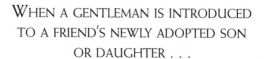

WHEN A GENTLEMAN IS INTRODUCED TO A FRIEND'S NEWLY ADOPTED SON OR DAUGHTER . . .

He does not say:

"Don't worry. He'll start looking like you after a while."

"Look out! You'll probably get pregnant right away."

"Are you going to tell her she's adopted?"

"Aren't you kind to give a poor orphan a home."

But he does say:

"Congratulations. He's a very lucky boy, and you're a lucky mommy and daddy too."

The adoption of a child of any age is—or should be—an act of love and a cause for celebration. In such situations, an enlightened gentleman does not pass along old wives' tales. Instead, he readily joins in the rejoicing, presenting the child with a gift if he feels the urge to do so.

WHEN A GENTLEMAN LEARNS THAT TWO OF HIS FRIENDS PLAN TO BE MARRIED—AND THE GENTLEMAN FEELS THAT THEY ARE IN FOR BIG TROUBLE . . .

He does not say:

"I certainly hope you folks have a pre-nup."

"Why don't you just try living together first?"

"Let me give you the name of my lawyer. You're probably going to need it."

But he does say:

"That's great news. Have you set the date?"

Even if he feels that a marriage is doomed from the start, a gentleman does not go around predicting its failure. The bride-and-groom-to-be might share interests of which he is not aware; they might have redeeming traits that are not evident; or they might, very simply, be in love. Now is the time for the gentleman to keep his opinions to himself. If the marriage should fall apart, no one will want to hear him saying, "I knew it would never last."

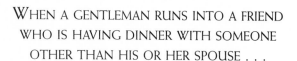

WHEN A GENTLEMAN RUNS INTO A FRIEND WHO IS HAVING DINNER WITH SOMEONE OTHER THAN HIS OR HER SPOUSE . . .

He does not say:
"So, where's Marsha? Home with the poodle?"
"Let me guess: This is your niece. Right?"
"Don't worry. My lips are sealed."

But he does say:
"Hello, Jim (or Susan), how's your dinner?"

The time is long past when husbands and wives could only be seen in public—or in social situations—with their spouses. In fact, a gentleman may assume that if his friend is being seen in public with an acquaintance other than his or her spouse, nothing illicit is afoot. He may feel free to introduce himself to his friend's escort, should his friend neglect that casual nicety.

IF A GENTLEMAN'S AQUAINTANCE CONFIDES IN HIM THAT HE OR SHE IS HAVING AN AFFAIR . . .

He does not say:

"Well, have fun, but don't get caught."

"I knew you'd get tired of Missy (or Morrie) eventually."

"You're not trying to drag me into this, are you?"

"Why are you telling me this?"

But he does say:

"You're my friend, Tammy (or Tommy), but this is something you'll have to work out for yourself."

A gentleman does not involve himself in other people's love triangles. He neither takes sides, nor does he tell tales. He knows that in the heat of passion Tammy or Tommy might not be thinking rationally. He also knows that at least one of the three people in the triangle will be hurt. There might come a time when he can forestall some of the damage, but until that time comes, if a gentleman is wise, he will pretend that he and his friend never had this particular conversation.

When an Acquaintance Reveals to a Gentleman that He and His Wife Are Taking Fertility Drugs . . .

He does not say:

"Couldn't you just adopt? Think of all the unwanted children out there."

"That's an awful lot of money to spend just to have a baby."

"Which of you has the problem?"

"Watch out! You could end up with a litter."

"If God had wanted you to have children . . ."

But he does say:

"Well, good luck, Larry. I'll be looking forward to the blessed event."

A gentleman never passes judgment on this sort of highly personal decision. Nor does he try to make light of the situation. It is clearly a weighty decision that will have long-lasting effects. He wishes them well and resists all temptation in coming months to ask, "How's the baby making going?"

WHEN A GENTLEMAN'S FRIEND
ANNOUNCES THAT HE OR SHE IS
GETTING A DIVORCE (OR SEVERING
A LONGTIME RELATIONSHIP) . . .

He does not say:

"Who's having the affair?"

"Who's getting the Lexus?"

"I told people this would never work out."

"I know somebody who's perfect for you."

"How about dinner and a movie on Friday?"

But he does say:

"I'm sorry to hear that. Are you doing okay?"

In such situations, the gentleman's friend
might feel sorely abused. The last thing he or
she might want is a dating service. A gentleman
need not attempt to fix the problem; he need
only demonstrate compassion and offer a
listening ear. If both parties in the breakup
happen to be his friends, and if there seems to
be no reason to lay blame at anyone's doorstep,
he makes a special effort to avoid taking sides.

WHEN A FRIEND REVEALS TO A
GENTLEMAN THAT HE AND HIS CURRENT
LOVE INTEREST MET VIA THE INTERNET . . .

He does not say:

"Be careful. I've heard horror stories about
Internet love affairs."

"Don't tell too many people about this. They'll
think you are a loser."

"Did the two of you have cybersex?"

But he does say:

"That's interesting. Are the two of you having fun?"

Meeting via the Internet has come to seem
no more curious than meeting on a blind date
or through a personal ad in the newspaper. A
gentleman might not think this is the wisest
way to seek companionship, but he knows not
to waste his breath giving warnings in regard to
affairs of the heart.

WINING AND DINING

WHEN A GENTLEMAN IS PAYING FOR
DINNER AND HIS GUEST SUGGESTS
ORDERING THE MOST EXPENSIVE BOTTLE
OF WINE ON THE MENU . . .

He does not say:

"Whoa! Have you forgotten who's paying for this?"

"Okay, but it means you can't have dessert."

"Guess nobody's ever gonna call you a cheap date."

But he does say:

"I was thinking about having one of the Californias;
They're a little more within my price range."

This response can prevent a great deal of
embarrassment—either later in the evening, or
later in the month when the gentleman
discovers that he cannot pay his credit card
bill. It also suggests that the gentleman has a
straightforward, trusting relationship with his
guest. It is important, however, that the
gentleman initiate this dialogue by asking,
"What were you thinking of ordering?" at a
moment when the server is not hovering at
the table. If the server returns before the
gentleman establishes the limits, he
unapologetically asks for more time.

WHEN A GENTLEMAN AND HIS GUESTS EXPERIENCE POOR SERVICE IN A RESTAURANT . . .

He does not say:

"How many times do I have to ask you for a glass of water?"

"Can't you get anything right?"

"I guess you don't know who I am, do you?"

"You just blew your tip, buddy."

"No. I *do not* want a complimentary scoop of ice cream."

But he does say:

"We seem to be having a problem here. Would you point out the manager for me, please?"

A gentleman does not get into arguments at the dinner table with anyone—least of all with a server who is supposed to be making sure he has a hassle-free evening. When it is clear that he is not getting the level of service that he expects, a gentleman goes to the manager or, at the very least, the host. If that person cannot solve the problem, or at least find another server, the gentleman has learned an important lesson and does not take his business to that restaurant again.

When a gentleman has offered to pay for dinner and his credit card is rejected . . .

He does not say:

"Your machine must be screwed up."

"Run it through again. I know I mailed the payment."

"You know, this happens to me all the time."

But he does say:

"Excuse me a moment. I'll be right back."

If they are dining in even a moderately fine restaurant, both the servers and the management will do everything possible to help avoid embarrassment in this situation. Ideally, they will find an excuse to call him away from the table before giving him the bad news. If there really is a problem with his account and there is no other way of temporarily settling the bill (perhaps by running to a nearby ATM or convincing the restaurant to accept a check), as a last resort the gentleman might have to beg assistance from his would-be guests. Even then, the gentleman does not blame others, and he never, never creates a scene.

WHEN A GENTLEMAN DISCOVERS THAT HIS
DINNER PARTNER HAS SOMETHING STUCK
BETWEEN HIS OR HER TEETH . . .

He does not say:
"Don't you need a toothpick?"

"That cheese sauce really sticks to the old caps,
doesn't it?"

"You saving that little bit of spaghetti for a
midnight snack?"

But he does say:
"You might want to use your napkin. You have a
little bit of spinach stuck to one of your teeth."

A gentleman alerts his friend, even his
girlfriend, the minute he notices an offending
leftover morsel. No one wants to discover that
he or she has gone through two cups of after-
dinner coffee and a cognac with a strand of
spinach stuck between his or her incisors.

When a Gentleman Learns That a Friend Is Beginning a Diet . . .

He does not say:

"This isn't one of those crazy, all-protein things, is it?"

"You? You don't need to lose weight!"

"Are you on another diet? Why don't you just give up?"

"You know, I was just thinking you needed to drop a few pounds."

But he does say:

"Good luck. I really admire your willpower."

A gentleman realizes that self-image is an entirely personal matter. He also knows that a huge percentage of Americans are technically overweight. It is not his place to judge anyone's motivations in beginning a diet. Nor does he dismiss their efforts, no matter how many times they may have tried before. Because he is a gentleman, he provides support and encouragement in any friend's drive for self-improvement.

WHEN A GENTLEMAN IS IN THE COMPANY
OF A FRIEND OR ACQUAINTANCE WHOSE
ACTIONS ARE PROVING EMBARRASSING . . .

He does not say:

"Mike, I'd like to come back here again some time. But I'm certainly not bringing you."

"I hope you know you're making a fool of yourself."

"Everybody, I hope you'll forgive Meg for the way she's acting."

"Meg? I don't know anybody named Meg."

But he does say:

Nothing—at least not in front of other people, and not unless the friend's behavior threatens to cause a disturbance.

When a friend is behaving rudely, a gentleman has a couple of options: He may take the friend aside and suggest that the friend temper his or her behavior. Or he may simply tough it out, knowing that he need never spend time with this person again. Under no circumstances does he apologize for another person's behavior; neither does he attempt to embarrass another person in front of others.

ON THE JOB

When a gentleman gets a promotion, and a coworker does not . . .

He does not say:

"I told you you should have chipped in on the boss's Christmas present."

"Guess the cream always rises to the top."

"Bet you wish you hadn't bought that new BMW."

"I could use some coffee. How about making a pot?"

But he does say:

"Joe, I'm looking forward to our continuing to work together. Let's grab some lunch."

If a gentleman and his friend have both been considered for the same promotion, it is foolish to pretend that once one of them has moved up the ladder business can simply proceed as usual. A gentleman may choose to say nothing specific about his good fortune, but he must continue to be cordial to his friend and associate. If the friend appears to be unduly glum in the wake of the gentleman's promotion, the gentleman may simply, and privately, ask the tough question, "Joe, is there a problem between us because of my new job?"

WHEN A COWORKER GETS A PROMOTION, AND THE GENTLEMAN DOES NOT . . .

He does not say:

"Well, you certainly brown-nosed your way into that one, didn't you?"

"I hope you don't think I'm taking orders from you."

"You'd better look out, buddy. I'm watching your every move."

"Guess this means you're buying lunch."

But he does say:

"Congratulations, Bob. I'm here to help out with whatever you need."

A gentleman might feel that he has, in truth, been cheated out of a job that was rightfully his, but he knows that once a decision has been made, he must live with it. If he feels he cannot continue to be happy having been passed over for a particular promotion, he starts looking for a new job. In no case does he attempt to sabotage a coworker. Envy and revenge are ugly. What's worse, they are inevitably self-destructive.

WHEN A GENTLEMAN NEEDS TO BREAK OFF A
TELEPHONE CONVERSATION WITH A LONG-
WINDED BUSINESS ASSOCIATE OR FRIEND . . .

He does not say:
"I need to run. I've got something more important
to do."

"Is this going to take much longer, Laurie?"

"Can you hold a sec?" (and then cut off the caller).

But he does say:
"I wish I had time to continue our conversation, but
I've got a meeting (or a lunch appointment, or a
deadline) in a half hour. Now, what was the point
you wanted to make?"

A gentleman need not apologize for
gracefully ending a phone conversation that has
gone on too long. Unless his business is
customer service, he is not required to have his
day taken up by intrusive callers. At the same
time, a gentleman remembers what it is like to
be on the other end of the phone. He attempts
to complete his telephone business as
expeditiously as possible.

When a gentleman's intimate friend or coworker has chronic bad breath . . .

He does not say:

"What crawled into your mouth and died?"

"Don't you think it's time for you to see the dentist?"

"You don't kiss Peggy Sue with your breath smelling like that, do you?"

But he does say:

"I have these new breath mints. Maybe you'd like to try one."

Halitosis can impede the social (and professional) life of an otherwise wonderful person. So a gentleman is actually doing a kindness by letting his friend know that the problem exists. (The friend, after all, seldom smells his own breath.) If the friend declines the gentleman's offer of a breath mint, the gentleman is perfectly right to insist, saying, "Actually, Tommy, I think you need one." If the friend's problem persists, and if he has not taken the hint, the gentleman might wish to try the breath-mint exercise again.

WHEN A COWORKER TELLS A
GENTLEMAN THAT HE OR SHE IS
BEING TREATED FOR DEPRESSION OR
SOME OTHER MENTAL ILLNESS . . .

He does not say:

"Does the boss know about this?"

"Did they start you on pills yet?"

"You're not having to see a shrink, are you?"

"I understand. This place drives me crazy too."

"Don't worry. I won't breathe a word."

But he does say:

"Thank you for telling me about this. If I can help
in any way, please let me know."

Mental illness is no longer considered a
reason for shame and need not be suffered in
silence. When a coworker tells the gentleman
about his condition, he might very well be
taking a step toward recovery. Unless his fellow
employee volunteers further details, a
gentleman does not ask for them. Although he
does not treat the coworker's revelation as if it
were a dark secret, he resists all temptation to
spread the news among others in the office.

IF A GENTLEMAN FEELS UNCOMFORTABLE WHEN HE IS ASKED TO CONTRIBUTE TO A GIFT FOR A COWORKER . . .

He does not say:

"Why should I give her a baby present? What's she ever given me?"

"You other guys may be pushovers, but you can count me out."

"If I want to give somebody a present, I'll do it myself."

But he does say:

"Thanks for asking, but Marjorie and I hardly know each other at all."

A gentleman need not act like a curmudgeon when declining to participate in group gifts. As long as he makes it clear that he bears no ill will against the recipient of the proposed gift, he is perfectly justified in stating his position—and sticking to it. By refusing to chip in on the gift, however, he also forfeits his share of the cake and ice cream at the coffee-break baby shower.

WHEN A GENTLEMAN ARRIVES MORE THAN TEN MINUTES LATE FOR A MEETING . . .

He does not say:

"Sorry. I got hung up on some really important business."

"I can't believe you went ahead without me."

"Mind if we go back to the top of the agenda?"

But he does say:

Nothing if the meeting is already under way, keeping his apologies at a minimum until the group's business is finished.

A tardy gentleman does not expect the world to wait for him. If he makes a habit of being late for appointments, he understands that the business world will probably proceed without him. If he is a central participant in the meeting, he makes a special effort to be punctual. When he has an opportunity to apologize for his tardiness, he does so, without going into needless detail but making sure to add, "I appreciate your going ahead without me."

WHEN A GENTLEMAN IS ASKED TO GIVE A
JOB RECOMMENDATION FOR A FRIEND OR
COWORKER WHO HE KNOWS IS NOT
EQUIPPED TO DO THE JOB . . .

He does not say:

"That's not a job you want, is it?"

"You know I'll have to tell the truth, don't you?"

"Sorry, I don't recommend just anybody."

"I'm sorry, I have my reputation to think about."

But he does say:

"Larry, let me be frank. I don't think this is the job
for you."

If the friend presses the gentleman to
explain what he means, the gentleman may
choose to be either straightforward or
compassionately evasive. He may choose to
explain that he does not feel that his friend
currently has the experience or the skills to
handle the new job's responsibilities, or he may
simply explain that he does not feel that his
friend will like the work environment in the
new office. In either case, he has escaped the
awkward, unproductive task of writing a tepid,
lackluster letter of reference.

WHEN A GENTLEMAN LEARNS THAT A FRIEND HAS QUIT HIS OR HER JOB . . .

He does not say:

"Maybe you should have waited. It's always easier to find a new job while you're still working."

"You know, jobs like that one aren't a dime a dozen."

"Are you going to sign up for unemployment?"

"I hope you didn't burn too many bridges."

But he does say:

"That had to be a tough decision, but I know you had to do what was right for you."

Not all career decisions are made on the basis of money. Although his friend might have had a great salary and wonderful benefits, the gentleman might not be aware of the stress taking its toll. While his friend is out of work, a gentleman may do what he can to encourage him to relax and chart a new course. It won't hurt, either, to take the friend out to lunch every now and then.

WHEN A FRIEND OR COWORKER ASKS A
GENTLEMAN TO SUPPORT A POLITICAL
CANDIDATE WHOM THE GENTLEMAN
STRONGLY OPPOSES . . .

He does not say:

"What do you think I am, a Nazi?"

"Do I look like a tree-hugger?"

"I wouldn't vote for that fool if my life depended
on it."

But he does say:

"Thanks for asking, Ginny, but your man [or
woman] just isn't my cup of tea."

Unless a gentleman is ready to spend an
hour in a heated political debate, he will want
to get out of this situation as quickly as
possible. He knows that if his friend is involved
enough to be soliciting the gentleman's vote,
there is little point in the gentleman's
attempting to explain his reasons for supporting
the opposition. He remembers that ours is a
free country and uses his time more wisely,
attempting to sway undecided voters.

WHEN A GENTLEMAN FINDS HIMSELF
IN THE COMPANY OF FRIENDS OR
COWORKERS WHO BEGIN TELLING OFF-
COLOR JOKES . . .

He does not say:

"You think that's funny? Did you hear the one
about . . . ?"

"You'd better be glad Miriam's taking a smoke break.
If she heard you, she could get you canned."

"Gosh, George, I didn't know you were such a bigot!"

But he does say:

"Guys, jokes like that are not funny. Isn't there
something else we could laugh at?"

A gentleman is not required to be an officer
in the politically correct army, but he does
make a habit of thinking of others and trying to
put himself in their place. He knows that there
are plenty of humorous topics that do not
offend and that, however supposedly well-
meaning, jokes that target and stereotype
minorities and ethnicities divide, rather than
unite, the office—and even the world.

WHEN A FRIEND OR A COWORKER ASKS A GENTLEMAN TO TELL A LIE . . .

He does not say:

"You must have really messed up something bad."

"What's it worth to you?"

"You know lying is a sin don't you?"

But he does say:

"No. I'm afraid I can't do that."

Nothing more needs to be said.

WHEN A GENTLEMAN WISHES A FRIEND
OR COWORKER TO LEAVE THE ROOM,
SO THAT HE CAN CONTINUE A
CONVERSATION IN PRIVATE . . .

He does not say:
   "Okay, Seth, you've got to go now. We've got
   important business to do."

   "Uh, Jim, can't you take a hint? Beat it."

   "Freddy, don't I hear your mother calling?"

But he does say:
   "Alex, Jim and I have one more issue we need to
   discuss. Would you mind giving us a few
   minutes alone?"

A gentleman attempts to make it clear that
his friend or coworker is not being excluded
from a high-powered, top-secret meeting. The
gentleman remains absolutely casual when
asking his friend to leave the room, thereby
allaying any fears that the friend will be the
topic of the closed-door conversation. If, in
truth, the gentleman does need to discuss a
matter related to his friend, he does so at an
entirely separate meeting. Whatever the topic
of the private conversation, he keeps it short.

WHEN TO USE FIRST NAMES

Although the world today is for the most part on a first-name basis, a gentleman knows it is always safe to address a new acquaintance as "Mr." or "Ms." He especially follows this rule of thumb if the new acquaintance is an older person or if he is dealing with his superior in a business environment. However, once Ms. Jones has told him, "Please call me Mary," a gentleman concedes to her wish. Otherwise, he runs the risk of making her feel ill at ease.

As a general rule, if a gentleman finds that a peer is referring to a person as "Mr. Brown" or "Ms. Smith", he may logically assume that that person wishes to be referred to as "Mr." or "Ms." He does not attempt to force business acquaintances to act as if they were his personal friends.

AFFAIRS OF THE HEART

WHEN A GENTLEMAN IS TURNED DOWN FOR A DATE . . .

He does not say:

"Okay, then what about *next* Friday?"

"What's the matter? Am I being too pushy?"

"But I thought you said you *liked* pro wrestling."

"Well, you certainly don't know what you're missing."

"Bitch!"

But he does say:

"I understand. Maybe we can do something together some other time."

In affairs of the heart, a gentleman attempts, above all else, never to appear desperate. If he senses that he is being given the cold shoulder, he does not continue in pursuit of a person who has little interest in his attentions. If he does sense that there is hope for a second chance, he waits a few weeks and then tries again, making sure *not* to refer to his previous bad luck.

When a Friend Offers to Arrange a Blind Date for a Gentleman . . .

He does not say:

"It all depends. What does she look like?"

"If she's such a catch, why aren't you dating her?"

"What makes you think I need help getting dates?"

"Thanks, but I've seen the kind of women you date."

But he does say:

If he is interested, "Can you tell me a little bit about her, maybe some of her interests?"

If he's not interested at all, "I'm sure she's a great person, but blind dates just aren't my thing."

A gentleman might enjoy the adventure of blind dating, or the accompanying anxiety may give him the hives. Either way, he attempts to be gracious to a friend who is, at least in the friend's opinion, trying to do him a favor. Whatever his opinion of blind dates in general, he can feel complimented that his friend thinks he's a nice guy who deserves a little romance in his life.

WHEN A GENTLEMAN IS ASKED TO
ARRANGE A DATE BETWEEN TWO
FRIENDS, AND THE GENTLEMAN IS
CONVINCED IT IS A ROTTEN IDEA . . .

He does not say:

"Listen, he (or she) is out of your league."

"You're too good for her (or him)."

"I understand he (or she) has really bad B.O."

But he does say:

"Sorry, friend, I don't play matchmaker."

If he is wise, in this situation, a gentleman
sticks by his guns and proceeds to change the
subject. In that way, he avoids making excuses
and forcing himself to find an explanation,
however feeble, that does not hurt his friend's
feelings. In such matters, however, a gentleman
attempts to be consistent, knowing that, even in
the best of circumstances, playing Cupid is
dangerous business.

WHEN A GENTLEMAN IS SUBJECTED TO UNWANTED SEXUAL ADVANCES (AND IT *DOES* HAPPEN) . . .

He does not say:

"What kind of boy do you think I am?"

"Not tonight. I've got a headache."

"Why don't we just have another piña colada?"

"I thought we came here to talk."

But he does say:

"I think you are a very nice person, but I'm not interested in our having a sexual relationship."

The "you're a very nice person" line might sound trite, but it does soften the blow of the actual message. In this situation, the gentleman owes it to himself, and to the other person, to be absolutely frank. If the admirer will not take no for an answer, a gentleman has no recourse but to leave the premises.

WHEN A POTENTIAL LOVE INTEREST ASKS A GENTLEMAN TO REVEAL HIS SEXUAL HISTORY . . .

He does not say:
"Don't worry; I'm always careful."

"I suppose *you've* been Miss Goody-Two-Shoes."

"I'm not the type to kiss and tell."

But he does say:
"I believe in being honest, and I appreciate your asking. Here's the truth . . ."

A gentleman does not lie, especially in a situation that could save a life.

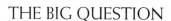

THE BIG QUESTION

When it comes to saying the right thing, there can be no more important decision for a gentleman than choosing the moment when he asks a lady to marry him. The moment may be highly dramatic, complete with a four-course dinner and the presentation of a diamond ring. Or it may come more quietly, during a walk on the beach. Either way, a gentleman knows that the timing must be right and that he must choose his words wisely. He must avoid any suggestion of "popping the question," as if he were only asking her to marry him as a brilliant idea that has come to him on the spur of the moment.

Whether he has thought to bring roses and an engagement ring, or whether his action is spontaneous, a gentleman says something like, "I've been thinking a lot about this lately, and I want you to know that I love you. I want us to be married, and I'm hoping that you feel the same way too."

A gentleman makes sure the lady knows that he wants this, the most important decision of their lives, to be a mutual one, the beginning of a lifetime of shared decisions.

AT A DINNER PARTY

WHEN A GENTLEMAN HAS DIFFICULTY UNDERSTANDING A PERSON WHO HAS A FOREIGN ACCENT—OR A SPEECH IMPEDIMENT . . .

He does not say:

"Isn't there some kind of sign language you people use?"

"What's the matter? Don't they speak English where you come from?"

"Wow. You must really have a hard time using the telephone."

But he does say:

"I hope you'll pardon me as I want us to be able to have this conversation, but I'm having a hard time understanding you."

This sort of remark suggests that it is the gentleman, not his new acquaintance, who has a problem. It also provides him with the opportunity, if there is a language barrier, to bring an interpreter into the conversation. If a speech impediment is involved, the gentleman may suggest that he and his acquaintance resort to pen and paper, hoping that, at future meetings, the gentleman will become better attuned to his friend's speech patterns.

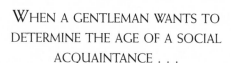

When a gentleman wants to determine the age of a social acquaintance . . .

He does not say:

"What year did you graduate from high school?"

"I bet you and I are about the same age, aren't we?"

"How far away are you from retirement?"

"If you were a tree, how many rings would you have?"

But he does say:

Nothing.

There are hardly any social circumstances which demand that a gentleman know another person's age. Only when the conversation is related to shared experiences—and when knowing a person's age might provide an interesting point of reference—should the subject even be broached. Even then, a gentleman is content with a general age range. No further specifics are required.

WHEN A FRIEND ASKS A GENTLEMAN
IF HE LIKES THE FRIEND'S NEW OUTFIT—
AND THE GENTLEMAN FINDS IT
UNATTRACTIVE . . .

He does not say:
   "I'll say this much: Not everybody can wear
   chartreuse."

   "It'll probably look better after you've lost a little
   weight."

   "Shopping on sale again, huh?"

But he does say:
   "You always look great. But I have to say, that
   blue shirt of yours is still my favorite."

A gentleman can avoid insulting his friend and, at the same time, extend a compliment on the friend's usual taste in clothes. What's more, by mentioning a specific item from the friend's wardrobe, the gentleman wins points for having paid attention.

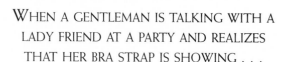

When a gentleman is talking with a lady friend at a party and realizes that her bra strap is showing . . .

He does not say:

"Oh, I see we're shopping at Victoria's Secret these days."

"What's the matter, Helen; did you get dressed in the dark?"

"Completely color-coordinated. Hmmm. I like that in a woman."

But he does say:

"Louise, I probably should tell you your strap is showing."

Any lady, no matter how stuffy her upbringing, will appreciate a gentleman saving her from embarrassment. Of course, a gentleman may only break this sort of news in the most delicate manner possible, perhaps by whispering it discreetly in the lady's ear. In no case, unless he and the lady are on the most intimate terms, does he attempt to rearrange her lingerie himself. This is, in most cases, a minor operation that she can handle quite capably without his assistance.

WHEN A GENTLEMAN REALIZES THAT THE
MAN TO WHOM HE IS SPEAKING IS WEARING
A NEW HAIRPIECE—OR HAS OBVIOUSLY
JUST HAD IMPLANT SURGERY . . .

He does not say:

"Hey, isn't there something different about you?"

"Can you wear that thing in the pool?"

"Guess you couldn't take Rogaine."

"You know, a lot of women really like balding men."

But he does say:

"It's good to see you, Chris. How are things at the
store?"

No matter how many people insist they
find balding men sexy, such compliments offer
little compensation for a man who is losing his
hair. To improve his self-image, he might go to
great lengths and expense. Such decisions may
appear superficial, but they stem from deeply
rooted insecurities. If a new toupee or a hair-
weave makes a man feel better, it has
accomplished its purpose. Unless he is asked for
his opinion in such situations, a gentleman
keeps his opinions to himself.

WHEN A GENTLEMAN ENCOUNTERS AN
ACQUAINTANCE TO WHOM HE HAS BEEN
INTRODUCED REPEATEDLY AND CANNOT,
FOR THE LIFE OF HIM, REMEMBER THE
PERSON'S NAME . . .

He does not say:

"Tell me again how to pronounce your last name."

"I'm having an Alzheimer's moment."

"I meet so many people; obviously some names
are going to slip my mind."

But he does say:

"It's great seeing you, but you have the advantage
on me here. I'd appreciate it if you'd remind me
of your name again."

A gentleman knows that, in this situation, it is
best to bite the bullet and admit that he's having a
memory lapse. If he tries the "Tell me how to
pronounce your last name" ploy, the name almost
invariably will be Smith, or worse yet, it will be
the same as the gentleman's. Acquaintances might
laugh off an occasional gaffe, but if a gentleman
habitually forgets the person's name, he may need
to try a little harder.

WHEN A GENTLEMAN IS BEING
ENTERTAINED AT THE HOME OF A FRIEND,
AND HE DISCOVERS THE FOOD IS
VIRTUALLY INEDIBLE . . .

He does not say:

"Yuck!"

"Does this shrimp taste kinda funny?"

"Just exactly what did you do to the rice?"

"Let me guess: This is the first time you've made this."

But he does say:

Nothing, unless his host or hostess brings up the subject.

If a gentleman is lucky in this situation, there will be *something* edible on his plate, even if it is just a carrot curl. That way, he can at least appear to be having dinner, but in no case does he force himself to consume food that he fears might make him ill. If his host or hostess notices that he is not eating, he admits, unashamedly, that something is wrong. Most likely, the host or hostess will realize the food is bad, and everybody can head to the kitchen for peanut butter sandwiches, or skip ahead to dessert.

WHEN A GENTLEMAN DISCOVERS THAT A FRIEND HAS SERVED HIM A DISH WHICH HE CANNOT EAT—BECAUSE OF DIETARY CONCERNS, MEDICAL REASONS, OR RELIGIOUS CONVICTIONS . . .

He does not say:

"You don't expect me to eat this stuff, do you?"

"Don't you know what they do to baby calves to make veal?"

"Well, I'm certainly glad I'm not hungry."

"Sorry, I forgot to tell you: I'm fasting this week."

But he does say:

"Sally, I'm afraid I'm allergic to shellfish. But I'd love an extra serving of the salad, if it's available."

If his host or hostess has not alerted him ahead of time to the evening's menu, a gentleman with special dietary requests might be caught off guard. In such situations, he has every right—in fact, he has an obligation—to explain why he is not touching the entrée. He is frank and undramatic when explaining his dietary needs. If his host or hostess provides an alternative dish that is appropriate, he accepts it gratefully and, if possible, cleans his plate.

IF A GENTLEMAN, AT A PARTY, LEARNS
THAT A FRIEND PLANS TO START A
BUSINESS, AND THE GENTLEMAN IS
CONVINCED IT WILL BOMB . . .

He does not say:

"Well, crazier schemes have worked."

"You know, almost 75 percent of all new businesses fail."

"I certainly hope you've got some strong investors."

"Do you have a backup plan?"

But he does say:

"Best of luck, Kathryn. You've got an ambitious plan, and you're certainly in for an adventure."

A gentleman need not pass judgment on a friend's dreams, no matter how ill-fated he might think they are. A remark such as this allows a gentleman to wish his friend good luck (because he does want the best for his friends), without predicting success or failure. It also prevents the gentleman from having any right in the future to say, "I told you so."

HOW TO MAKE A TOAST

Over the course of his life, a gentleman will probably be invited to any number of wedding receptions, anniversary dinners, birthday parties, and other festive events. At some point, almost inevitably, he will be asked to make a toast, and if he is asked, he must not refuse. However, he need not attempt to give an after-dinner speech or perform a stand-up comedy routine.

His tribute may be something as simple as, "Joe, I'm proud to call you my friend." He may choose to share some memory of his friendship with the honoree, or if he is confident of his skill as a humorist, he may toss off a lighthearted quip. In no case does he attempt to embarrass the guest of honor. Neither does he ramble on at length. A gentleman remembers that because toasts usually come late in the evening the wisest course is always to be succinct.

AT A COCKTAIL PARTY

WHEN A FRIEND OR ACQUAINTANCE COMPLIMENTS A GENTLEMAN'S NEW SHIRT . . .

He does not say:

"What? This old thing?"

"Well, you should like it, considering how much I paid for it."

"Thanks a lot. I'll let you wear it some time."

But he does say:

"Thank you. I appreciate you telling me that."

Although a gentleman might think he is acting humble, he is actually being rude when he declines to accept a compliment. Such responses suggest that he questions the taste of the person offering the compliment. If he chooses to do so, he may even reinforce his friend's opinion by saying, "Thank you. This is the first time I've worn it. It's a color I really like."

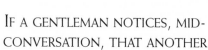

IF A GENTLEMAN NOTICES, MID-CONVERSATION, THAT ANOTHER GENTLEMAN'S FLY IS OPEN . . .

He does not say:

"Look out, Bob, the barn door's open."

"So, I see Mary Jane gave you red silk boxers for Valentine's Day."

"You know, you could get arrested for walking around that way in Utah."

But he does say:

"Jim, your fly is open."

There is no greater kindness one man can pay another than to alert him, as quickly as possible, in this awkward situation. As in the case of a lady whose lingerie strap is showing, this is a problem that can be—and should be—quickly taken care of right on the spot. A gentleman does not make a scene or attempt to get a laugh when alerting his friend that his pants are unzipped. If the two men are talking with a group of friends, he may simply place his hand on his friend's shoulder and draw him aside, tell him the news, and then let the evening proceed as if nothing has happened.

WHEN A GENTLEMAN, AT A PARTY, BUMPS INTO A FRIEND WHO OWES HIM MONEY . . .

He does not say:

"I can't believe you'd dare speak to me, considering the money you owe me."

"What do you think the folks here would say if they knew you owe me $500?"

"Hmmmm. Is that a new polo shirt?"

But he does say:

Nothing, at least not at that moment.

A gentleman knows that a party is no time to bring up difficult or unpleasant business. If he feels awkward in the company of his overdue debtor, he simply greets him in a mannerly way and then moves on. The next day, however, the gentleman has every right to contact his friend, saying, "I saw you at Laura and Mack's last night, Joe, and it reminded me of the deal we set up a while back. I'd appreciate getting it settled, since I have some expenses of my own coming up in the next couple of weeks." By this point in the transaction, the gentleman might have already lost a friend, but he has every right to get his money back.

IF A GENTLEMAN WISHES TO SMOKE AT THE HOME OF A FRIEND BUT DOES NOT FIND AN OBVIOUS PLACE TO DISPOSE OF HIS ASHES . . .

He does not say:

"Okay if I use this saucer for an ashtray?"

"Gee. I guess nobody much smokes around here."

"I'm just gonna have one. I'll put it out in the sink."

But he does say:

"I'd like to have a cigarette. Please excuse me while I step outside."

In today's clean-air-conscious world, a lack of ashtrays should be a signal to any observant gentleman smoker. He makes the offer to enjoy his smoke on a balcony, a porch, or a landing. If his host or hostess insists that he remain inside, he does not light up until a proper ashtray, or a suitable substitute, has been provided.

WHEN A GENTLEMAN, AT A COCKTAIL
PARTY, ENCOUNTERS A FRIEND WHO HAS
SUPPOSEDLY BEEN IN TREATMENT FOR
ALCOHOL OR DRUG ADDICTION . . .

He does not say:

"Hey, I thought you were on the wagon."

"I bet it's tough being around all this booze."

"Don't worry. I've got my eye on you. If you get into trouble, I'll drive you home."

But he does say:

Whatever he would normally say to a friend at a cocktail gathering.

A gentleman does not jump to conclusions or make hasty assumptions. His friend's presence at this party might indicate that his recovery program is working well. The gentleman need not assume that the liquid in his friend's glass is anything other than sparkling water. Until he has reason to think otherwise, he silently congratulates his friend on his bravery in tackling one of society's toughest problems.

WHEN A FRIEND AT A PARTY PRESSURES A
GENTLEMAN TO HAVE A COCKTAIL,
ALTHOUGH THE GENTLEMAN DOES NOT
DRINK ALCOHOL . . .

He does not say:

"Do you think I have to be drunk to have a good time?"

"What's the matter? Afraid to drink alone?"

"Okay. But just a small one."

But he does say:

"How about some soda? I don't drink alcohol."

A gentleman need not apologize for abstaining, no matter what his reason. He does not pass judgment on his drinking friends, nor does he allow them to pass judgment on him. He feels no compulsion to explain why he does not drink—whether for reasons of health, religion, or addiction. He simply states what he would like to drink and hopes that his host will be able to provide him with a refreshing non-alcoholic libation.

WHEN A GENTLEMAN, AT A PARTY, IS
INTRODUCED TO A WOMAN WHO IS
WEARING WHAT MIGHT VERY WELL BE A
MATERNITY DRESS . . .

He does not say:
  "I bet you'll be glad when that baby gets here."

  "When are you due?"

  "I didn't know that Georgia Tent and Awning
  made clothes."

But he does say:
  "Hello. It's a pleasure to meet you."

Whether a woman is pregnant or not, a
gentleman can still enjoy making her
acquaintance. If she is, in fact, pregnant, she
might be relieved to meet at least one person
who wants to talk about something other than
the impending arrival. What's more, the
gentleman might be relieved not to have to
make small talk about babies, a subject about
which he might know very little.

When a gentleman has been trapped with a boring guest at a cocktail party . . .

He does not say:
  "Do you know where to find the bathroom?"

  "No. I really am interested in quantum physics."

  "Did I just hear somebody say they've started a game of Twister in the sunroom?"

But he does say:
  "It's been nice talking with you, but I think I'd like to refresh my drink. Would you like to walk with me to the bar?"

In this way, the gentleman is making it clear that his conversation with his new acquaintance is swiftly approaching its close. (If he merely pretends to be headed for the bathroom, the bland conversationalist will probably still be there, awaiting his return.) Nevertheless, the gentleman is not abandoning his tedious friend. By leading him or her to the bar, the gentleman is providing ample opportunities to introduce his acquaintance to some other partygoer.

W HEN A GENTLEMAN HAS NEGLECTED
TO RESPOND TO A PARTY INVITATION
THAT WAS MARKED RSVP ("PLEASE REPLY"
IN FRENCH) . . .

He does not say:

"Hope you don't mind my calling so late. It just
slipped my mind."

"I figured it was a big party, so I just came ahead
anyhow."

"I *can't* be the only one who didn't call."

"What do you mean there's not a place for me at
the table?"

But he does say:

"Mary Jane, I hope you'll forgive me for calling so late.
I do hope you'll still have room for me at your party."

W hen a gentleman receives an invitation
marked RSVP, he replies as soon as he possibly
can. Even if he postpones calling until the last
minute, he still must swallow his pride and pick
up the phone. If the host or hostess should
happen to have filled her table without him, he
has no right to be upset. Instead, he might say,
"I understand. I hope you have a lovely evening.
I'll try to have better manners next time."

IF A GENTLEMAN'S HOST TELLS HIM HE IS IN NO CONDITION TO DRIVE HIMSELF HOME SAFELY . . .

He does not say:

"Tryin' to get rid of me, huh?"

"I feel just dandy. You get somebody to follow me, and I'll be great."

"A cab? I never take cabs."

"Just gimme another Scotch and I'll snap back in shape."

But he does say:

"Okay, take the keys. Somebody want to call me a cab?"

When a gentleman's friends tell him he has had a few too many cocktails, he believes them. They are, after all, his friends.

HOW TO ASK
FOR A DANCE

These days a gentleman seldom encounters a full-fledged ballroom dance. More often, a gentleman will glimpse a person in a club or at a social event whom he finds attractive and with whom, he hopes, a dance might be a convenient icebreaker, not to mention a romantic experience.

Easygoing though he may be, he does not just stride up and ask, "Hey, you wanna dance?" Instead, he works his way up to the question by breaking the ice with a few simple comments. If he receives any sort of encouragement, then, and only then, does he suggest, "I really like this song. How about you? Would you like to dance?" (He makes sure, of course, to select a song that makes the most of his dancing abilities, no matter how limited they may be.)

If the answer is "no," a gentleman takes "no" for an answer, but it does not necessarily mean that the object of his affection is not interested. He may simply be approaching a nondancer.

CUTTING IN

Cutting in" is a tradition that only makes sense on a traditional ballroom floor. At a dance club, with music blaring, the attempt will probably go unnoticed or, even worse, be deemed as evidence of inebriation. In such situations, a gentleman's only real option is to catch the attention of his hoped-for partner and say, "Sometime when you're free, I'd like it if we could have a dance." If he is in a situation where an orchestra is playing waltzes and where he may approach a dancing couple in a gracious manner, however, a gentleman may give the man a light tap on the shoulder, and ask, "Do you mind if I cut in?"

Tradition holds that unless the lady objects—which she should not do—the dancing gentleman must give up his partner. Once that dance is done, however, the gentleman must say, "Thank you," to the lady and return her to the man who gave her up.

THE HOST WITH
THE MOST

WHEN A GENTLEMAN RECEIVES A GIFT THAT IS THE DUPLICATE OF SOMETHING HE ALREADY OWNS . . .

He does not say:

"You know, when I bought my first one of these, I thought how much I'd really like to have two of them."

"I guess great minds think alike."

"You didn't happen to keep the receipt, did you?"

But he does say:

"What a great gift! I love it!"

In this situation, the gentleman can be honestly exuberant. His friend does indeed know the gentleman's taste—he knows it so well, in fact, that he's purchased just the sort of thing the gentleman would buy for himself. The best part is that, even after the gentleman has exchanged the duplicate gift, he can continue to use the original, and his friend will be none the wiser.

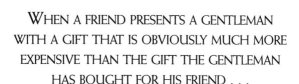

WHEN A FRIEND PRESENTS A GENTLEMAN
WITH A GIFT THAT IS OBVIOUSLY MUCH MORE
EXPENSIVE THAN THE GIFT THE GENTLEMAN
HAS BOUGHT FOR HIS FRIEND . . .

He does not say:
"Wow, you certainly made me look cheap."

"Of course, this is only part of your gift. The rest
of it hasn't come in yet."

"I really hate show-offs."

But he does say:
"Thank you. What a beautiful gift."

When a gentleman has received a
particularly generous gift, he may be as effusive
as he likes in expressing his gratitude, but he
knows that his friend would be made
uncomfortable if the gentleman were to
apologize or appear embarrassed about the less
expensive gift he has presented. He trusts that
his friend appreciates his gift for the sentiment
it expresses—not for the size of its price tag.
Gift-giving is not a competition sport. Because
gifts are a sign of generosity and appreciation,
whenever they are offered, everybody wins.

WHEN A GENTLEMAN OPENS HIS PRESENT
AND DISCOVERS THAT IT OBVIOUSLY COST
MUCH LESS THAN THE ONE HE PURCHASED
FOR HIS FRIEND . . .

He does not say:
  "Little things mean a lot."

  "I'm always impressed with what you can do with
  five dollars."

But he does say:
  "Thank you. What a lovely gift."

A gentleman does not rate gifts on the size
of their price tags. He does not, in fact, rate
them on any basis. He knows that his friend
may have invested many hours in selecting even
the simplest gift. He would never belittle that
effort. To do so would imply that he selects his
friends on the basis of their annual incomes.

WHEN A GENTLEMAN REALIZES THAT A
FIGHT IS BREWING BETWEEN TWO FRIENDS
AT A PARTY WHERE HE IS IN CHARGE . . .

He does not say:

"Why don't you guys just have another drink to
cool down?"

"That really was a dumb-ass remark, Jerry. If I
were Gary, I'd want to punch you out too."

"If you're gonna throw something, make sure it's
not that Ming Dynasty vase."

But he does say:

"Guys, If you don't quiet down, I'm going to have
to ask both of you to leave."

In such situations, particularly if alcohol is
involved, a gentleman does not take sides. His
primary concern is the safety of everyone
involved. If the argumentative friends will not
take a breather, the gentleman must stick by his
word and insist that they leave. Otherwise, they
will spoil the evening for themselves, the host,
and the other guests. When they leave,
however, the host makes sure they have safe
transportation home.

When a friend lights up a cigarette in a gentleman's smoke-free home . . .

He does not say:

"What are you trying to do . . . kill us all?"

"You can smoke up your own house if you want to, Jason, but get that stuff out of my house."

"Do you see any ashtrays around here, Barbara? Can't you take a hint?"

But he does say:

"Jason, you'll find an ashtray out on the balcony. I keep it there for my friends who smoke."

A gentleman has the right to live in a smoke-free home, but he might want to entertain smokers in his home from time to time. Once they are his guests, he would never attempt to insult them. Thus, he plans ahead, thinking of his friends' convenience and—as much as possible, in inclement weather—their health.

WHEN A GUEST BREAKS A PIECE OF CHINA
(OR A VASE OR A GLASS) AT A PARTY WHERE
A GENTLEMAN IS HOST . . .

He does not say:

"Do you know what a plate like that *costs?*"

"Luckily, you can buy me a replacement at
Nordstrom's."

"The least you can do is start cleaning up the mess."

"Next time, I'm using Chinet."

But he does say:

"Are you all right, Marvin? I hope you didn't cut
yourself."

When a gentleman entertains regularly, he
quickly learns that broken china and glassware
are a part of life. When a plate or a glass gets
broken, he expresses concern for the welfare of
his guest, not for the loss of the dinner plate or
goblet. If the guest should offer to pay for the
breakage, the gentleman refuses the offer. If his
china is more important to him than his friends,
he dines alone.

WHEN A GENTLEMAN REALIZES THAT HE
HAS PREPARED A DINNER THAT IS, FOR
WHATEVER REASON, INEDIBLE . . .

He does not say:

"I hope you don't mind if it's a little burned. You
can scrape off the crusty bits."

"I'm sorry this tastes like this. You're lucky there's
a McDonalds on the way home."

"Does it taste strange to you? It tastes perfectly
fine to me."

But he does say:

"Who likes pepperoni?"

Even the most meticulous gentleman makes
mistakes, and, because he is a gentleman, he
admits them readily. If he has burned the
chicken, or if the pork chops taste funny, he
knows he does not have to cancel his party.
Instead, he immediately orders take-out, for
which he, of course, picks up the tab. That way,
he will be remembered for his grace under fire,
not for a night in the emergency room.

WHEN A GENTLEMAN HAS PREPARED
DINNER AND LEARNS THAT A FRIEND—FOR
WHATEVER REASON—CANNOT EAT THE
FOOD HE HAS COOKED . . .

He does not say:

"It won't make you really sick will it?"

"I wish you'd told me you don't eat shellfish. I
wouldn't have spent all that money on these shrimp."

"So what if you're a vegetarian? Fish isn't meat."

But he does say:

"I'm sorry, Barbara. I should have mentioned what I
was planning to serve. Can I give you a little more
salad?"

In today's society, no gentleman should be
surprised to discover that a friend—for whatever
reasons—may decline to eat certain foods. When
extending a dinner invitation, he should suggest the
menu he has in mind, hoping that his friend will let
him know if it includes something he or she cannot
eat. If that is the case, he reworks his menu, or at
the very least he provides alternatives. If, however,
he discovers too late that his friend cannot eat the
lovingly prepared dinner, the gentleman does his
best to come up with a quick substitute.

WHEN A GENTLEMAN OPENS A GIFT THAT HE ABSOLUTELY ABHORS . . .

He does not say:
"Well, it's definitely not something I would have bought for myself."

"Where does somebody find something like this?"

"You shouldn't have. I *really* mean it."

But he does say:
"Thanks so much. I've never seen a coffee mug quite like this before."

Whenever possible, a gentleman does not open his gifts in the presence of their givers. (That way he avoids having to disguise his dismay at receiving a gift that is absolutely wrong for him; better yet, he avoids the possibility of opening duplicate gifts from two friends.) When he is forced into the ceremonial unwrapping of gifts, however, he must be prepared for surprises, not all of them pleasant. He may feel free to exchange any gift that he has no use for, but when he opens any package, he must honestly mean it when he says, "You are wonderful to give me this. I'm lucky to have you as a friend."

WHEN A GENTLEMAN, AS HOST OF A
PARTY, REALIZES THAT ONE OF HIS GUESTS
HAS HAD TOO MUCH TO DRINK . . .

He does not say:

"Finish that drink while I make a pot of coffee."

"Don't leave until I can find somebody to follow you."

"Man, if you don't realize how drunk you are,
you've got a real problem."

But he does say:

"Jerry, you've had plenty to drink, and I'm
concerned about your safety. Just to be safe, give
me your keys; we're going to get you a cab home."

A gentleman does not attempt to reason
with a friend who has been overserved. Instead,
the gentleman takes charge, accepts no
arguments to the contrary, and makes sure his
friend gets home safely. (Sending another
partygoer to tail the drunk driver accomplishes
absolutely nothing.) The friend might protest
and even become confrontational. But in the
morning, or at least by the next afternoon, he
will be grateful. Better yet, he will be alive.

WHEN A GENTLEMAN HAS NO CHOICE BUT
TO TAKE AN IMPORTANT PHONE CALL
WHILE ENTERTAINING FRIENDS OR
CONDUCTING A BUSINESS MEETING . . .

He does not say:
"You folks don't mind if I take this call, do you?"

"Keep yourselves entertained. I'd better catch this one."

"Don't listen to this. Just talk among yourselves."

"I know this is rude, but I'm gonna do it anyway."

But he does say:
"Excuse me, please. I need to take this call. I'll try
to make it quick."

When a gentleman says he'll keep it quick,
he tries to do just that. He does not engage in
lengthy social calls while his guests are cooling
their heels in the living room. On rare occasions
there might be emergencies or heat-of-the-
moment business calls that require a gentleman's
immediate attention, but those are the only times
he is justified in abandoning his friends or
business associates in order to talk on the phone.
In all cases, if he must take this sort of call, he
does so in another room. That way, the party—
or the meeting—can continue in his absence.

WHEN A GENTLEMAN IS HOSTING A PARTY, AND THE NEIGHBORS COME KNOCKING AT THE DOOR . . .

He does not say:

"Oops. Guess I should have warned you."

"Noisy? Duh—it's a party."

"If you can just stick it out for a while, they'll be leaving around 1 A.M."

"Aw, come on in. Have a beer."

But he does say:

"I'm sorry. We'll quiet down."

One of the built-in responsibilities of urban life is the necessity to remember the neighbors. When planning a get-together of any size, a gentleman should alert the folks next door, as well as the folks across the hall. If an unplanned gathering springs up, especially after hours, a gentleman makes sure it does not get out of hand by monitoring the sound system and the level of laughter. If the neighbors have felt the need to complain, the gentleman must comply with their wishes, and he must apologize in the morning.

WHEN A GENTLEMAN IS HOSTING A
SEATED DINNER PARTY AND AN INVITED
GUEST CALLS TO ASK IF HE MAY BRING AN
ADDITIONAL FRIEND, FOR WHOM THE
GENTLEMAN DOES NOT HAVE ROOM . . .

He does not say:

"How dare you ask such a thing?"

"Okay, but he's got to bring his own steak."

"Bring him along, but it's going to make
everybody very uncomfortable."

But he does say:

"I'd love for you to bring Jim [or Jessica], but I'm
afraid I've only got room at the table for eight."

When a friend calls with this kind of
request, he should expect that he will get this
kind of response. A gentleman tries to plan his
parties so that everyone has a good time. He
knows whether there is room at his table for an
extra plate. If an extra chair would cause
everyone to be knocking elbows, he does not
attempt to crowd in an extra body.

WHEN A GENTLEMAN FEELS IT IS TIME TO CHANGE THE TOPIC OF THE CONVERSATION AT A PARTY . . .

He does not say:
   "Enough about that. Let's talk about Graham's new mustache."

   "I hate to interrupt you, Gloria, but before I forget it, I wanted to tell my new joke."

   "Are you people as bored with this conversation as I am?"

But he does say:
   "This might not be exactly on the subject, but your comment reminds me of something I read the other day in the *New York Times*."

Because he is a skillful conversationalist, a gentleman is adept at guiding table talk. If a less creative guest continues to return to the exhausted topic, the gentleman may persevere, interjecting when possible, "Yes, but don't you think it's interesting that. . . ." But if a gentleman feels that the tenor of the conversation is growing tasteless or potentially incendiary, he has every right to say, "I think maybe we should talk about something else."

HOW TO MAKE AN INTRODUCTION

Even in our increasingly casual society, a gentleman respects the time-honored traditions surrounding social introductions.

- A younger person is always introduced to an older person. For example, when Tim Lyons, who is in his twenties, is introduced to Mr. Allgood, who is in his fifties, a gentleman says, "Mr. Allgood, I'd like you to meet Larry Lyons." Even if a younger woman is being introduced to an older man, a gentleman makes sure to say the older person's name first.

- When a gentleman introduces a man and a woman who are of essentially the same age, he introduces the man *to* the woman. Thus, if his friends Sally Baldwin and Larry Lyons do not know each other, a gentleman introduces them by saying, "Sally, this is my friend Larry Lyons." Then the gentleman turns to Larry and says, "Larry, this is Sally Baldwin."

- In all cases, a gentleman feels free to add some detail to stimulate conversation. He

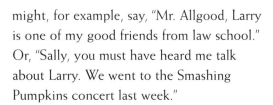

might, for example, say, "Mr. Allgood, Larry is one of my good friends from law school." Or, "Sally, you must have heard me talk about Larry. We went to the Smashing Pumpkins concert last week."

- When being introduced to a young boy, a gentleman makes the offer of a handshake. If the boy has not had practice in the art of handshaking, the gentleman simply gives him a pat on the shoulder and says, "It's awfully nice to meet you, Sam."

- A gentleman makes every effort to pronounce names clearly. If it is convenient, he repeats the names at some not-too-distant point in the conversation.

Even if he is uncertain of the protocol of the moment, however, a gentleman always does his best to make an introduction. Even if he makes a small mistake, he has not committed the more serious error of being rude.

HOW TO START A
CONVERSATION

At a party, a reception, or a business meeting, a gentleman strikes up a conversation with any pleasant person he encounters. To prevent awkwardness, however, he begins with positive, noncontroversial subject matter. He might say, "This is a nice party, isn't it?" or "Charlie has certainly done a good job of bringing this meeting together, hasn't he?"

In every case, a gentleman begins by asking a question that does not bring the conversation around to himself. If the person standing next to him responds cordially, he continues with a few more questions until the conversation is under way. He might venture out by asking, for example, "Did you catch the Pirates game last week?" But he knows that he is still testing the waters.

Never, or at least not until the conversation is well under way, does he venture into uncharted territory, such as the lukewarm food on the buffet or the recent downslide in the company stock. Invariably, after he has made this sort of comment, a gentleman discovers that he is speaking to the hostess's sister or the boss's son.

HOW TO END A CONVERSATION

A gentleman recognizes that every conversation has its own natural rhythm. He is not being rude or inconsiderate when he attempts to bring any conversation—no matter how pleasant or important—to a timely close.

When talking on the telephone, a gentleman accepts the responsibility for ending any conversation he has begun. When the conversation is taking place in his office, it is the gentleman's responsibility to bring the meeting to a close. In every case, he states as directly as possible that it is time for the discussion to end; he does not allow the conversation to dawdle along uncomfortably. On the telephone, he might say something as simple as, "It's been very good talking to you, Jack. I hope we get to talk again soon." In person, he stands up, thanks his guest for meeting with him, and extends his hand for a handshake.

PRIVATE LIVES

WHEN A GENTLEMAN'S EVENING IS INTERRUPTED BY A TELEMARKETER . . .

He does not say:

"How does it feel to spend your life irritating people?"

"Give me your home number. I want to call you tomorrow night when *you're* trying to have dinner."

"Is this the only job you could get?"

But he does say:

"No thanks. Don't call me again. Good night."

Telemarketers, for good or ill, are simply doing the job they were hired to do. A gentleman does not attempt to insult them. A gentleman does not intentionally make people feel bad but is always polite and courteous, even with those who may be annoying. He simply dismisses them as quickly as possible and returns to his dinner.

WHEN AN ACQUAINTANCE ASKS A
GENTLEMAN HOW HE CAST HIS VOTE, AND
THE GENTLEMAN WOULD PREFER TO KEEP
THAT INFORMATION PRIVATE . . .

He does not say:

"As long as its a free country, I don't have to
tell you."

"It's none of your damn business!"

"Why do you want to know? You probably don't
think I voted."

But he does say:

"I prefer not to talk about my vote."

No matter what the gentleman's response,
his acquaintance will probably assume that the
gentleman has either been on the losing side in
the election or that, at the very least, he has
voted against the acquaintance's candidate. There
is no avoiding such assumptions. The gentleman
can, however, prevent reigniting an argument
over an election that has already been decided.

WHEN AN ACQUAINTANCE ASKS A GENTLEMAN HOW OLD HE IS, AND HE PREFERS NOT TO DISCUSS HIS AGE . . .

He does not say:
"How old do you think?"

"How old do I look?"

"Why are you asking?"

But he does say:
"Sorry, but I don't give out that information."

A gentleman may make this sort of response in a lighthearted manner and still let it be known that he wants to talk about something else. More often than not, when a friend asks a gentleman's age, he intends, eventually, to offer a compliment. Still, for whatever reasons, a gentleman has the right to keep any of his vital statistics to himself.

WHEN A FRIEND DROPS BY UNANNOUNCED
AND A GENTLEMAN IS NOT IN THE MOOD
FOR—OR PREPARED FOR—COMPANY . . .

He does not say:

"I've got the flu. Go away; I don't want you to catch it."

"What the hell are you doing here?"

"Didn't your mother teach you any manners?"

But he does say:

"Thanks for dropping by, Jerry, but this is a bad time for me. Give me a call, and we'll get together sometime soon."

A gentleman feels no obligation to invite an unexpected guest into his home. Otherwise, he will be stuck with the dilemma of finding a gracious way to get him to leave. The gentleman should suggest that the unwanted guest give him a call to set up their next meeting, suggesting he wants to see the guest, just not right then.

WHEN AN ACQUAINTANCE ASKS A GENTLEMAN TO REVEAL HIS SALARY . . .

He does not say:

"Not as much as I'm worth."

"That's none of your business."

"What a tacky question!"

But he does say:

"I prefer not to talk about salaries."

A gentleman makes it clear that he does not discuss *anyone's* personal income. (Otherwise, his nosy acquaintance is likely to pursue the issue, saying, "If you tell me your salary, I'll tell you mine.") A gentleman knows that his salary is part of a confidential agreement between him and his employer. If he is wise, he will keep it that way. Without fail, once he has revealed how much he makes, someone will feel that he is being overcompensated, while others will pity him for being paid so little.

WHEN A GENTLEMAN MUST SAY *NO* TO AN
ACQUAINTANCE WHO DOES NOT SEEM TO
GET THE MESSAGE . . .

He does not say:

"You know, begging is really, really unattractive."

"How stupid are you? Don't you know what the word *no* means?"

"Hugh, you're starting to piss me off, big time."

But he does say:

"Sammy, I said *no*. And that's my final answer on that subject."

When an acquaintance probes for personal information or asks a gentleman to participate in an inappropriate activity, the gentleman does not waffle. He says *no* early in the discussion, not giving tempers a chance to rise and allowing the conversation to move on to another topic.

When a thoughtless shopper attempts to cut in line ahead of a gentleman at the grocery store . . .

He does not say:

"Are you blind? Can't you see I'm standing here?"

"If you expect to see that bag of cat litter again, I'd suggest you get out of my way."

"Hey, wait a minute, little lady."

But he does say:

"Excuse me, but the end of the line is right here, behind me."

A gentleman stands up for his rights in situations such as these. If the intruder is purchasing only a few items, the gentleman may relent and allow him or her to go ahead, but even then he may say, "All right, since you have only a few items, I'll let you cut in." If the pushy shopper has a full cart and a handful of coupons, the gentleman is fully justified in standing his ground. In fact, he must do so, for the sake of any future shoppers who may encounter this annoying interloper.

WHEN A GENTLEMAN, ON AN AIRPLANE,
TRAIN, OR BUS IS SEATED NEXT TO A
FELLOW TRAVELER INTENT ON HAVING A
CONVERSATION . . .

He does not say:

"Can't you see I'm trying to sleep [or read, or
listen to my CD player]?"

"That's a fascinating story. Maybe the guy in the
aisle seat would like to hear it."

"Sorry, I'm not feeling well. I've got the flu."

But he does say:

"I wish I were able to talk with you, but I have to
finish this paperwork [or reading this article]
before the end of the flight."

When travelers are seated beside one another
on an airplane, they are not required to—or even
expected to—establish a social relationship. If a
gentleman and a fellow traveler are in the mood
to talk, they may enjoy each other's company. But
the gentleman feels no obligation to become best
friends with his temporary next-door neighbor. If
the two of them do strike up a conversation,
however, they talk quietly, so as not to disturb
other passengers.

GIVING, LENDING,
BORROWING,
AND SHARING

WHEN A GENTLEMAN IS APPROACHED BY A PANHANDLER, AND THE GENTLEMAN CHOOSES NOT TO GIVE HIM MONEY . . .

He does not say:

"Why don't you get a job?"

"Sorry. All I've got is a hundred-dollar bill."

"Do you think I'm crazy? I know you're just a drunk."

"Here, take this religious tract."

But he does say:

Nothing, unless he knows the address of a nearby homeless shelter

A gentleman should decide ahead of time for himself whether he wishes to give money—in even small amounts—to panhandlers. (In some cities, local governments discourage such giving, asking that donations go, instead, to coordinated relief efforts, such as the Salvation Army.) If a gentleman chooses to give to a panhandler, he does so discreetly, simply saying, "You're welcome," when he is thanked for his generosity.

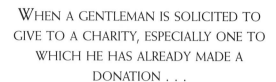

WHEN A GENTLEMAN IS SOLICITED TO
GIVE TO A CHARITY, ESPECIALLY ONE TO
WHICH HE HAS ALREADY MADE A
DONATION . . .

He does not say:

"Aren't you people ever satisfied?"

"Just wait until it's my turn to collect for the
Community Trust drive. You'll have to pay back then."

"Just tell me this: How much did you give?"

But he does say:

"No, Sue, I've given as much as I'm comfortable
giving to that cause right now."

A gentleman's personal finances, including
his charitable donations, are an absolutely private
matter—known only to him, his accountant, and
the IRS. When he is asked to contribute to a
worthy cause, he may turn it down and expect
that no questions will be asked. On the other
hand, if he does not think the cause is worthy, he
may feel free to ask that he not be solicited
again, explaining his decision in the briefest,
least confrontational manner possible.

When a gentleman learns that a friend has filed for bankruptcy . . .

He does not say:

"I thought you were flying pretty high there for a while."

"I hope you're going to learn from this."

"Don't you feel like a jerk, skipping out on your bills?"

"Now you know why I never lent you any money."

But he does say:

"That's a tough decision to make, Jack, but it will help you get on with your life."

A gentleman realizes that everyone must put his past mistakes and failures behind him. The option of bankruptcy might be abused in some cases, but in others it is truly a last resort. When a friend has come to this juncture, a gentleman does not add insult to injury. On the other hand, unless he has the wherewithal to do so, he does not volunteer financial assistance. In this case, he is very careful about saying, "Let me know if there is anything I can do to help."

WHEN AN ACQUAINTANCE ASKS A
GENTLEMAN HOW MUCH HE'S PAID FOR AN
ITEM OF CLOTHING OR SOME OTHER
PERSONAL PROPERTY . . .

He does not say:

"Why are you asking?"

"I can't believe you'd ask that."

"Probably more than you could afford."

But he does say:

"Gee, I'm not sure I remember."

Whether this response is accurate or simply a means of escaping an awkward situation, it will probably prevent any further probing. If the nosy acquaintance continues to push, saying, "Oh, come now, that sweater must have cost $750," a gentleman might simply close the discussion by saying, "I'm sorry, but I'd rather not talk about that."

WHEN A GENTLEMAN RECEIVES AN
UNEXPECTED HOLIDAY GIFT FROM A FRIEND FOR
WHOM HE HAS NOT BOUGHT A PRESENT . . .

He does not say:

"What are you doing giving me a present? I didn't get you anything."

"I already got your package. I just haven't had time to get it wrapped."

"Golly, I feel like dirt."

But he does say:

"Thanks. Aren't you kind to think of me?"

Gifts are supposed to be given as tributes, not in hopes of recompense. If a gentleman receives an unexpected gift, he accepts it in the kindest way he can manage. He need not attempt to come up with a gift in return after the fact. Instead, he makes sure to write an especially gracious thank-you note. If he wishes, he may make a point of remembering his generous friend when the next holiday season rolls around, but in truth, he need only be grateful and make good use of his gift.

When a gentleman's friend asks to borrow money, and the gentleman does not feel comfortable making the loan . . .

He does not say:

"What do I look like—an ATM?"

"Guess you shouldn't have bought those Gucci loafers, eh?"

"What makes you think I've got that kind of money?"

"What's the matter? Bank turn you down?"

But he does say:

"I'm sorry you're having a tough time, Simon, but I just make it a practice not to lend money to my friends."

A gentleman has every right to keep, spend, lend, or give away his money as he pleases. He tries, however, to be sensitive to the needs of a friend who is in a hard spot. He does not probe into the friend's troubles; neither does he make demeaning or humiliating remarks. Instead, he simply states his policy and sticks to it.

WHEN A FRIEND ASKS TO BORROW A
GENTLEMAN'S FAVORITE HAMMER OR
PUTTER OR SWEATER AND THE GENTLEMAN
WOULD PREFER NOT TO LEND IT FOR FEAR
IT WILL NOT BE RETURNED . . .

He does not say:
   "Sorry, but I'm sort of picky about the people I
   lend my things to."

   "Don't you know what that thing cost?"

   "Are you sure you'll bring it back?"

But he does say:
   "I wish I could help you, Evan, but I just don't
   lend my tools. It's one of my private rules."

A gentleman does not openly question his
friend's integrity. If he prefers not to run the risk
of never having his hammer, his putter, or his
sweater returned, he simply does not lend it.
When he says this is his rule, whether it relates
to lending money or lending personal property,
he sticks to it, not favoring one friend over
another.

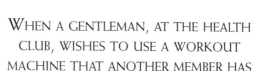

WHEN A GENTLEMAN, AT THE HEALTH CLUB, WISHES TO USE A WORKOUT MACHINE THAT ANOTHER MEMBER HAS BEEN MONOPOLIZING . . .

He does not say:

"Are you gonna hog those weights all day?"

"Why don't you free up that machine for somebody who *really* knows how to use it?"

"I'm in a real hurry. Just how many reps are you gonna do?"

But he does say:

"While you're resting between sets, how about if I cut in? Then, maybe we can switch off."

In any gym or health club, there are times when there is not enough equipment to go around; and, unfortunately, those are the times when boorish club members usually choose to work out. The best a gentleman can do is to offer to share the equipment, perhaps by offering to "spot" him or her on the next set of reps. If the loutish club member's behavior continues, a gentleman may wish to report him or her to the management. He does not force the issue in the middle of the workout room.

IN TIMES OF SADNESS

WHEN A GENTLEMAN'S COWORKER HAS RETURNED TO WORK AFTER THE DEATH OF A LOVED ONE . . .

He does not say:

"Gee, I guess your work really stacked up while you were away."

"I wish my aunt would die so that I could take a day off."

"Were you close?"

"Were you in the will?"

But he does say:

"I am sorry to hear about your uncle. Please let me know if there's anything I can do to help you get back into the swing of things here at work."

A gentleman might spend most of his waking hours with his coworkers, but he does not attempt to intrude into their private lives. He does not attempt to compare his family experience with theirs, either. His task as a well-mannered fellow employee is to assist his friend in achieving the easiest possible reentry at the workplace. In doing so, he provides great comfort.

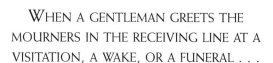

WHEN A GENTLEMAN GREETS THE
MOURNERS IN THE RECEIVING LINE AT A
VISITATION, A WAKE, OR A FUNERAL . . .

He does not say:
"I guess you must actually be relieved."

"Charlie really hung on, didn't he?"

"Maybe your life can get back to normal now."

"Well, as they say, only the good die young."

But he does say:
"I'm so sorry about your loss. I've been thinking about you a lot."

In times of grief, a gentleman is wise to keep his comments simple, honest, and heartfelt. When a friend has lost a child or a beloved parent, words, no matter how eloquent, cannot possibly fill the void. The friend might be confused by futile attempts to find sunshine behind the clouds, but he will retain memories of the gentleman's sturdy handshake and, if appropriate, his warm embrace.

WHEN A GENTLEMAN VISITS THE
FUNERAL HOME TO PAY HIS RESPECTS TO
THE FAMILY OF A DECEASED FRIEND AND
FINDS THAT THE FAMILY HAS ASKED THAT
THE CASKET REMAIN CLOSED . . .

He does not say:
   "Was he messed up that bad?"

   "Are you going to let us see the body later?"

   "Gee, I really wanted to see him one last time."

But he does say:
   Nothing. At least nothing related to the casket lid.

In some regions of the country, particularly
the South, open-casket funerals were once the
matter of course. That is no longer the case,
and open caskets are not even permitted in
some religious traditions. In this situation, no
matter how troubled a gentleman might be by
his questions, he keeps them to himself.

WHEN A FRIEND HAS LOST A BABY . . .

He does not say:

"You're still young. Aren't you glad you can have more children?"

"It was meant to be."

"This was God's way of saying you weren't ready."

"It was probably for the best. Kids are so much work."

"Well, at least you already have one child."

But he does say:

"I've been thinking about you," or if he is a praying person, "I want you to know you've been in my prayers."

It is pointless, and even cruel, to attempt to rationalize such a tragedy. In such situations, a gentleman edits his words meticulously. Even if he has experienced a similar sadness, he does not urge his friend to relive his or her anguish. A close friend will let the gentleman know when he or she is ready to talk about this devastating experience. Until then, a gentleman expresses his sympathy in the simplest and most sincere manner possible.

WHEN A FRIEND'S PET HAS DIED . . .

He does not say:
   "Did you have to put him to sleep?"

   "Well, he was pretty old for a dog."

   "Aren't you glad you can get a new puppy?"

   "I can't believe how upset you are. After all, it was just a cat."

But he does say:
   "I'm sorry about Fluffy. I know she meant a lot to you."

Whatever his opinion of pets—and pet owners—a gentleman knows that many people love their animals as much as (and sometimes more than) their human families. A gentleman does not make light of the loss of a beloved animal; neither does he suggest that an adored companion can be easily replaced. For some pet owners, such a remark is as heartless as suggesting that a husband or a wife can be easily replaced.

WHEN A LOVED ONE OF A GENTLEMAN'S FRIEND OR COWORKER HAS COMMITTED SUICIDE . . .

He does not say:

"But he always seemed so *happy*."

"That is so selfish."

"Now, I certainly hope you don't think this is your fault."

"You didn't find the body, did you?"

"Did she leave a note?"

But he does say:

"I'm so sorry to hear about Tom. Please know I've been thinking about you."

This is exactly the same comment a gentleman makes whenever a friend has lost a loved one, whatever the cause. The added trauma of suicide need not be theatricalized. Neither is it the gentleman's task to raise troubling questions. His friend is probably already searching for the very same answers.

WHEN A GENTLEMAN LEARNS THAT THE
DECEASED LOVED ONE OF A FRIEND OR
COWORKER HAS BEEN CREMATED . . .

He does not say:

"I couldn't do that."

"What did his parents say?"

"I'm not sure that's right. My religion doesn't allow it."

"Don't you feel sorta weird, having Sam's ashes right there in the house?"

But he does say:

"I wish I could have made it to the funeral. I understand it was a lovely service."

A gentleman's personal opinion about cremation is of no importance—unless he is having to decide upon a loved one's form of burial, or unless he is planning his own funeral. Some religious traditions do not permit cremation, but it is increasingly accepted as an option in many mainline faiths. The choice of cremation says nothing about the esteem in which the dearly departed was held.

WHEN THE LOVED ONE OF
A GENTLEMAN'S FRIEND OR
COWORKER HAS BEEN KILLED IN AN
AUTOMOBILE ACCIDENT . . .

He does not say:

"I bet she wasn't wearing her seat belt, was she?"

"Do they think the wreck was his fault?"

"How fast was he going?"

"Was there alcohol involved?"

"I certainly hope the other guy had insurance."

But he does say:

"This is a horrible blow, Mary. Please know that
you are in my thoughts."

Unless he is working as an officer of the
law, a gentleman does not ask probing questions
at such a sensitive time. Neither does he make
assumptions about guilt or innocence. He
simply expresses his concern in the most direct
way possible.

When a Gentleman Greets the Boyfriend or Girlfriend of the Deceased at a Memorial Service . . .

He does not say:

"Don't you wish now that you'd gotten married?"

"Guess you're glad now you didn't tie the knot."

"You're young. You'll find somebody else right away."

"Are you going to sit with the family at the service?"

"Do you know if you were in the will?"

But he does say:

"I'm sorry, Jill (or Jerry). You and Jerry (or Jill) were such a wonderful couple."

A gentleman never presumes that he knows all the details about the personal relationship of two other people. Especially in a time of grief, he does not probe for information, nor does he discuss what might have been. More important, he does not assume that, because no legal documents were signed, a boyfriend or girlfriend was not as cherished as a church-sanctioned spouse. The pain is just as real.

AWKWARDNESS
EXTRAORDINAIRE

When a gentlemen visits a friend in the hospital . . .

He does not say:

"Getting plenty of Jell-O?"

"You know, this is the hospital where my Uncle Bill died."

"How long is the insurance company going to let you stay?"

"Mind if I sit here and watch the game?"

But he does say:

"I was just passing by and thought I'd drop off this book. I enjoyed reading it and thought you might like it too."

A gentleman knows that people go to the hospital because they are sick, not because they need entertainment. He keeps his visits short and upbeat, avoiding topics—such as the health insurance system—that might lower his friend's spirits. He also avoids all jokes about Jell-O. After twenty-four hours in a hospital, his friend has heard them all.

WHEN A FRIEND SHOWS A GENTLEMAN
A PICTURE OF HIS NEW CHILD OR
GRANDCHILD, AND THE BABY, AT
LEAST IN THE GENTLEMAN'S OPINION,
IS LESS THAN ADORABLE . . .

He does not say:
   "Yikes!"

   "I bet his mother's crazy about him, isn't she?"

   "Don't worry. They grow out of that stage really
   quickly."

   "Well, that sure is a baby."

But he does say:
   "Gee, Leslie, I'll bet you're really proud."

Truth to tell, few babies look their best in
their neonatal photos. A gentleman will be wise
to proceed cautiously, even in the best of cases,
sticking to vapid exclamations of admiration
such as "Isn't she cute?" or "Look at those tiny
little fingers!" In such cases, as long as "she"
does not turn out to be a "he," a gentleman can
never go wrong.

When a gentleman encounters a friend shopping for birth control . . .

He does not say:

"Looks like somebody's about to have some fun."

"You're doing some wishful thinking, aren't you?"

But he does say:

"Hello, Rodney. How are you doing?"

There is no reason for a gentleman to mention or make light of a friend's purchase no matter what he or she is purchasing. Neither does a gentleman act as if he has discovered his friend making a street corner deal for heroin. Unless he is asked for advice in this situation, as should be the case in most situations, a gentleman keeps his personal preferences to himself.

WHEN A GENTLEMAN'S CLOSE LADY FRIEND ASKS IF SHE LOOKS FAT (AND SHE DOES) . . .

He does not say:

"No, actually I thought you lost weight."

"Who am I to ask? Look how much weight I've gained."

"Maybe it's just those slacks."

"Why worry? Some guys like their women sort of chunky."

But he does say:

"You're a great-looking woman (or a beautiful one, if he means it). If you've gained a little weight, you've got the style to carry it off."

A gentleman should never lie, and the truth of the matter is, when a lady friend asks this question, she already knows the answer. She's the one who checks the scales every morning; she's the one who just struggled to fit into the size eight jeans that fit perfectly a couple of weeks ago. The kindest, and most honest, course is to offer reinforcement and reassurance. A gentleman knows that that sort of response will never come back to bite him.

When a gentleman's unmarried woman friend tells him she is pregnant and plans to keep the baby . . .

He does not say:

"Well, gee, Gloria, don't you think a child should have two parents?"

"Do you know who the father is?"

"What's the matter? Couldn't you get him to marry you?"

But he does say:

"Congratulations. You'll make a wonderful mother."

If his friend is spreading the news of her pregnancy, a gentleman may assume that she is not ashamed of her condition. He greets her news with the same good wishes he would offer any expectant mother. The mother-to-be is probably well aware of the challenges before her; she does not need him to remind her.

WHEN A GENTLEMAN MUST BREAK A
SOCIAL COMMITMENT . . .

He does not say:

"I'm sorry, Anne, but I won't be able to make your party. Something more important has come up."

"Sorry, Chuck, we've got to reschedule dinner. Ralph just called with tickets to the hockey game."

But he does say:

"I'm sorry, Anne, but I can't make it on Friday evening. The boss just gave us a deadline for Monday, and it means no playtime this weekend. I hope you'll let me have a raincheck."

There are times when a gentleman must change—or cancel—his plans. In no case, however, does he cancel a social obligation simply because something more appealing has come up. When he calls to express his regrets, he clearly states his *actual* reason for bowing out, such as a death in the family or unexpected illness. He apologizes straightforwardly, and, if appropriate, attempts to reschedule the outing.

When it is necessary for a gentleman to make an apology . . .

He does not say:

"I understand you think I owe you an apology."

"Sorry if I hurt your feelings."

"Sometimes people just don't know when I'm joking."

"Boys will be boys."

But he does say:

"Miles, I'm sorry if I offended you the other evening when I commented on your Raiders jacket. I'd had a few beers and was a bit too rowdy."

A gentleman makes it clear that he understands an apology is in order—even if he truly meant no offense. He neither acts as though he is being coerced into apologizing, nor attempts to downplay any embarrassment or discomfort he might have caused. Once he has apologized, he does not raise the subject again. To do so is to reopen a gradually healing wound.

When a gentleman is
offered an apology . . .

He does not say:

"I guess you expect me to believe you really mean it."

"All right, but don't let it happen again."

"I'm sorry isn't good enough."

But he does say:

"I appreciate your apology, Bert. I was offended, I admit. Now let's just move on."

Unless a gentleman has been offended repeatedly by the same person, he accepts an apology at face value. He does not pretend that the offense never happened, but he makes it clear that he has now put the awkwardness behind him. He might not fully forgive, or fully forget, but he does not dwell on past unpleasantness.

When a friend tells a gentleman that he is gay or that she is a lesbian . . .

He does not say to him:

"Well, that's fine. Just don't get any ideas about me."

"Funny, you don't act gay."

"As if everybody didn't already know."

He does not say to her:

"But you're so feminine."

"I bet the right man could change that."

"What a shame."

But he does say:

"I'm glad you feel comfortable telling me that, Tad or Tabitha."

A gentleman realizes that despite the tolerance of the day, even a good friend might hesitate before revealing that he or she is gay. Even if he does not approve of his friend's sexual orientation, the gentleman is glad that his friend has taken him into his confidence. He does not pry into the details of his friend's sex life any more than he would pry into the bedroom habits of his heterosexual friends.

WHEN A FRIEND TELLS A GENTLEMAN
THAT HIS OR HER CHILD (OR SIBLING) IS
GAY, AND THE GENTLEMAN IS NOT SURE
WHETHER THE FAMILY IS HAPPY ABOUT
THE REVELATION . . .

He does not say:

"Maybe it's just a phase."

"I always thought he [or she] was sort of an oddball."

"I'm so sorry. I know you always wanted
grandchildren."

"Well, at least you'll never have to hire a decorator."

But he does say:

"Michael (or Sue) is a wonderful person. That's
the thing that really matters."

Unless the friend presses him for further
discussion of the matter, a gentleman does not
offer his opinions or advice. If the friend seems
truly distressed by the news, a gentleman may
suggest that the friend talk with a minister or a
counselor. If the friend seems to be taking the
news with little distress, a gentleman may say, "I
hope things continue to go well." In no case does
he attempt to bring his personal moral convictions
into the conversation.

WHEN A GENTLEMAN'S FRIEND OR COWORKER HAS HAD A CHILD WHO IS PROFOUNDLY DISABLED . . .

He does not say:

"I bet this is really going to be tough on your marriage."

"Aren't you glad you already have little Bobby?"

"Are you going to put him in an institution?"

But he does say:

"It's great to see you. I hope things are coming along all right."

In a situation of this seriousness, a gentleman does not attempt to volunteer advice—even if he has had a similar experience. The best he can do is allow his friend or coworker to talk, if he or she chooses to do so. For the parents, the joy of having a child might easily outweigh the special challenges that lie before them, and in most cases, they will have the same experiences shared by all parents—loss of sleep, dirty diapers, and the presence of overly doting grandparents. A gentleman might focus on these experiences, letting the parents fill him in on the child's medical condition as—or if—they see fit.

WHEN THE LOVED ONE OF A GENTLEMAN'S
FRIEND OR COWORKER IS HAVING LEGAL
TROUBLE, OR IS EVEN IN PRISON . . .

He does not say:

"Are you going to go visit him?"

"Hold your head up. You're not the one who's guilty."

"What's it like in there? Is it like OZ?"

"Don't worry about what anybody else says. I'm still your friend."

But he does say:

"Have you had a chance to talk to Tobias? How's he getting along?"

A gentleman does not ignore the fact that a friend is going through difficult times. However, he does not sensationalize the situation, probing for details that he can then recycle through the rumor mill. He might want to add a comment such as, "I can only imagine how tough this is. Let me know what I can do to help." He might even offer to assist a coworker (from time to time, not on an ongoing basis) in keeping up with his or her workload.

When a gentleman's friend announces that his or her parents have been moved to a nursing home . . .

He does not say:

"Is it a good one?"

"I'll bet that made you feel guilty, didn't it?"

"Well, I'd certainly never do that to my parents."

"I hope my kids never do that to me."

"Didn't I see a story about that place on the news the other night?"

But he does say:

"How are your folks doing, Cynthia? Are they settling in all right?"

A gentleman might have no idea of all the factors that have led his friend to make this decision. Neither should he assume that the friend's parents are opposed to the move. He expresses his concern but otherwise keeps his opinions to himself. And he never adds to his friend's worries by sharing horror stories gleaned from the nightly news. If the friend cares about such stories, he is probably keeping up with them himself.

WHEN A GENTLEMAN IS ASKED TO SUBSTANTIATE A RUMOR . . .

He does not say:

"Let me put it this way: I'm not going to say yes, and I'm not going to say no."

"I think I know the truth, but I'd better not say it."

"Don't you have any better way to waste your time?"

But he does say:

"I'm not sure what the truth is about that, so I'd prefer not to say anything."

When he is asked to feed the rumor mill, a gentleman does not play games, coyly suggesting that he has information but prefers not to share it. Whether he actually is privy to the inside scoop or whether he only has an impression of the actual truth, he does not pass along opinion as if it were fact.

WHEN A GENTLEMAN FEELS HE HAS BEEN PAID A "LEFT-HANDED" COMPLIMENT . . .

He does not say:

"Thank you . . . I think?"

"Man, you need to work on your manners."

"I guess you meant that as a compliment."

But he does say:

"Thank you."

A gentleman tries to think the best of everyone. He realizes that not everyone is a silver-tongued orator, and he assumes that, however awkwardly expressed, a compliment is always offered with the kindest of intentions. In the same way that he would never correct another person's grammar in public, he does not question the motivation behind a quirky compliment. He accepts it for its good intentions and then moves on with his life.

When a gentleman catches a friend in an obvious white lie . . .

He does not say:

"Glad you're not Pinocchio. You'd have a twelve-inch nose right about now."

"Okay, prove it."

"You know you're lying."

"What kind of fool do you take me for?"

But he does say:

Nothing—unless the lie might cause harm to another person, or to the liar himself.

A "white" lie may be well-intentioned. A friend may say, "Bobby and I are really good pals," when the gentleman knows that his friend cannot abide Bobby's presence. Such remarks have little chance of causing damage and give the gentleman no excuse for embarrassing the small-time liar. He may, however, mention the remark to his friend in private. And he may also file the incident away, as a reminder when he is asked to trust his friend in the future.

WHEN A GENTLEMAN CATCHES A FRIEND
OR COWORKER IN AN OUT-AND-OUT LIE,
ONE THAT COULD HAVE SERIOUS
REPERCUSSIONS . . .

He does not say:

"Jeff, you know you're lying."

"I certainly hope the boss doesn't hear you say that."

"Where'd you get that information?"

But he does say:

Nothing—at least not in public.

If a gentleman is aware that his friend or coworker has lied, and that the lie could have a serious impact on other people, he does not let it slide. He does not seek a confrontation in front of others, but he does confront his friend in private, saying, "Paula, I've got serious questions about what you told Peter about the Goldfarb account." He may even feel the need to set Peter straight about Paula's misinformation. Without accusing her of lying, he may say, for example, "Peter, I'm not sure Paula had her facts straight . . ." A gentleman does not rat on his friends, but he also does whatever he can to avert an impending disaster.

WHEN A GENTLEMAN DECLINES
A SOCIAL INVITATION . . .

He does not say:

"Sorry, Kristy. I probably wouldn't be comfortable at your party. Sometimes your crowd makes me feel weird."

"Gee. Wish I could make it, but my favorite show is on TV that night."

"I'll have to see. I've got a lot of reading to do."

But he does say:

"I'm sorry, Herold, but I won't be able to make it. I've already got a commitment."

As a rule, a gentleman does not decline a social invitation unless he has a prior commitment. (Even if he is not fond of his would-be host's choice of friends, he can at least stop by for a few minutes to demonstrate his gratitude for being invited.) If there are serious reasons for his declining the invitation—he will be uncomfortable with the guests' behavior or with the presence of alcohol or drugs—he declines graciously, but firmly, without further elaboration. If the host pressures him, he may go ahead and express his feelings, but a television show is never a good reason.

WHEN A GENTLEMAN, IN A MOVIE
THEATER, IS SEATED IN THE VICINITY OF A
FELLOW TICKETHOLDER WHO REFUSES TO
STOP TALKING . . .

He does not say:

"Hold it down. Some of us are trying to watch the
movie!"

"Hey, you over there. Shut your trap!"

"SSSSSSSSSH!"

But he does say:

"Excuse me, please. I'm having trouble hearing the
movie."

Even this sort of gentlemanly effort is
useless if the gentleman is not seated relatively
close to the self-absorbed talkers. Since he does
not want to add to the disturbance by shouting
across a crowded theater, and especially if the
chattering persists, a gentleman has no recourse
except to report the problem to the manager or
to an usher. If the situation does not improve,
the gentleman has every right to leave the
theater and ask for his money back.

WHEN A GENTLEMAN, EITHER AT A
WORSHIP SERVICE OR AT A LIVE CONCERT
OR THEATRICAL PERFORMANCE, IS SEATED
NEAR A PAIR OF TALKERS . . .

He does not say:

"Don't you people have any respect for *anything?*"

"Is this the first time you've ever been to a concert?"

"Would you please shut up? I'm trying to listen."

"SSSSSSSSSH!"

But he does say:

"Excuse me, please. I'm trying to listen [to the show/concert/sermon]."

A worship service or a live performance is slightly different from a movie theater, since it does suggest a somewhat higher degree of propriety. Because a house of worship or a concert hall is not completely dark, it may also allow a gentleman to silence the talkers simply by catching their eye and placing a finger to his lips. If the chattering continues, however, he may have to seek the assistance of an usher—either to quell the disturbance or to find a new seat for himself.

LIFE AMONG THE UNGENTLEMANLY

The world has more than its share of thoughtless people. A gentleman knows that he is likely to encounter his share of thoughtless people—whether they are people who talk during movies, people who smoke in nonsmoking sections, or people who attempt to break line at the store.

When he encounters such persons, a gentleman takes a deep breath and remains calm. He knows that it is highly unlikely that an ill-bred person will profit from his giving them an on-the-spot sermon about manners. At most, he may say, "Excuse me, I believe this is a non-smoking section" or "Please quiet down, I'm trying to hear the movie" or "Pardon me, the line ends here."

If the brutish person's crude behavior is making life difficult for people in addition to himself, a gentleman may choose to seek the aid of a theater manager or the host of a restaurant or he may have to bear the behavior without complaint, knowing it's not worth a scene. He does not, however, seek to be the Sir Galahad of Good Manners. The poor behavior of others is not a problem he was put on earth to solve.

HANDS OFF

In some instances when he encounters bad manners or even dangerous behavior, a gentleman is wise to say nothing at all. When crude behavior is the result of drunkenness, for example, a gentleman is wise to stay out of the way. The same goes for dangerous drivers on the highway. A sensible gentleman does not engage an undisciplined driver in a *Rebel Without a Cause*-style standoff. Tales of "road rage" assaults are becoming more frequent, and nothing good ever comes of such instances.

Sometimes, the bravest thing a gentleman can say is, "Let's get out of here."

WHEN GOOD GUYS GO BAD

*Talking Your Way Out of Trouble
When You've Blown It, Big Time*

He may monitor his speech meticulously. He may say please and thank you. He may refuse to talk about politics at the dinner table. But once in a while, every gentleman, even the most scrupulous one, is going to put his foot in his mouth or commit a *faux pas* so ghastly that an apology may not be enough. A gentleman never intentionally offends another person, but of course sometimes he makes a mistake. The following are some instances of the sorts of moments that might doom even the most well-meaning gentleman to a lifelong diet of humble pie and examples of how he might possibly salvage the situation.

WHEN A GENTLEMAN HAS TRIED VERY HARD TO GIVE HIS SWEETHEART THE RIGHT PRESENT BUT IMMEDIATELY REALIZES HE'S GOT IT WRONG . . .

He is wise to admit his gaffe and plead for a little understanding. A gentleman's loved one may crave cookies dipped in peanut butter, but on a holiday or an important anniversary a case of cookies and a tub of peanut butter will simply never fill the bill. The gentleman may think he has been creative and observant, but those qualities will do him no good when his sweetie opens the package and bursts into tears.

In such cases, he may even beg for pity, saying, "I was trying to do something nice. I guess I just didn't do a very good job." He may even want to add, "Maybe I'll have to ask for guidance next time." He feels no need to apologize when he has done his best. But as soon as possible, he sends a peace offering—something that is always correct, like flowers, with a note that says, "I'll get it right next time honey; I promise."

Gentlemen can avoid these situations, of course, by remembering a few rules: 1) Never give anything that has a cord attached. 2) Never give your sweetheart anything she's ever seen on another woman. 3) Never give shoes, especially not galoshes.

WHEN A GENTLEMAN ASKS A NEW ACQUAINTANCE WHEN HER BABY IS DUE, AND IT TURNS OUT SHE'S NOT EVEN PREGNANT . . .

He swallows his pride and takes the blame. A gentleman can avoid such mistakes simply by avoiding all temptation to ask probing questions. In this situation, however, he has already overstepped his boundaries. His only way out is to say, right on the spot, "I guess I look like a fool, don't I? That's what I get for making assumptions." By doing so, he at least demonstrates that he knows how he should have behaved.

WHEN A GENTLEMAN REALIZES HE HAS SPENT TOO MUCH TIME TELLING HIS DATE ABOUT THE CHARMS OF ANOTHER WOMAN AT THE PARTY . . .

It will do absolutely no good for the gentleman to say, "Maybe if you'd been paying more attention to me, I wouldn't have been looking at Mary." His best course is to calm the waters by saying, "Well, yes, she is a good-looking woman, but she's not you. And you're the woman I've invited out this evening. Want to stop somewhere for a nightcap?" Then, over a latte or a brandy, he gives his full attention to his date for the evening and makes sure Mary's name never gets mentioned again.

WHEN A GENTLEMAN REALIZES TWO DAYS AFTER A HEATED ARGUMENT THAT HE WAS IN THE WRONG . . .

He shows his true mettle by admitting his mistake. Such an admission is, in fact, about the grandest possible demonstration of gentlemanly behavior. He need only say, "Sam, I've realized that you were right when we were talking about the national debt the other day. I was wrong. I should be more careful to get my facts right."

WHEN A GENTLEMAN, IN THE THROES OF PASSION, CALLS OUT A NAME, AND IT IS NOT THE NAME OF ANYONE WHO IS IN THE ROOM AT THE TIME . . .

He will have some explaining to do. Even in the most intimate of moments, a gentleman thinks before he speaks, because, even if he is not listening to himself, somebody else probably is. And that person may very well be taking notes. If he does flub in this truly horrifying manner, he can only say, "I don't know what came over me." If his partner forces the issue by asking, "Who's Veronica?" the gentleman saves a ghastly moment by turning it into a triumph, transforming a potential insult into an awkward, but still appealing, compliment. "Ah, Veronica," he says with a sigh. "I met her years ago, and she was the first

great love of my life. You're the only woman
I've ever met who made me feel that special." If
his love interest doesn't mind comparisons, even
complimentary ones, the gentleman may escape
with his life.

WHEN A GENTLEMAN HAS LOST HIS TEMPER
AND RAISED HIS VOICE TO HIS SECRETARY, HIS
ADMINISTRATIVE ASSISTANT, OR ANY OTHER
COWORKER . . .

In such cases, the gentleman can only pray
that he has not made any idle threats or given
any ultimatums. If he is lucky, he can get by with
a simple, honest apology. ("Forgive me for
yelling at you, Trudy. It was entirely out of line.
There was no excuse for my behavior.") If he has,
however, made statements he must retract, he
does so as soon as possible before they circulate
around the office. He sets the record straight as
clearly as possible saying, "I didn't mean what I
said about your salary the other day, Gibson. I'm
sorry. Please know that I value your work.

If a gentleman discovers that he is given to
rages or outbursts of temper, he will be well-
advised to consult a physician or a counselor.

WHEN A GENTLEMAN FINDS HIMSELF DOING
BUSINESS WITH A PERSON WHOSE INTEGRITY,
OR BUSINESS ACUMEN, HE HAS OPENLY
QUESTIONED IN THE PAST . . .

He is highly careful about any agreements
or deals that he signs—at least until his earlier
impressions have been proven wrong. He may
even put his feelings on the line, saying, "Pat,
you may know that I've had questions about
some your earlier dealings, so let's be
absolutely businesslike about our relationship."
If he has learned, however, that he has been in
error in his estimation of his new associate, he
clears the air as soon as possible, saying,
"Terrance, you may know that I've doubted
your integrity in the past. I've learned that I
was wrong. I hope we can work together now,
starting with a clean slate."

WHEN A GENTLEMAN HAS MADE HIMSELF,
AND HIS DATE, LATE FOR AN EVENT, SIMPLY
BECAUSE HE HAS REFUSED TO STOP AND ASK
FOR DIRECTIONS . . .

He must admit his apparent gender defect in
the failure to ask for directions. Many a man has
found himself a hundred miles away from his

destination, or going the wrong way on an unlighted country road at midnight, simply because he is determined he is genetically equipped with a homing device that renders unnecessary all maps, compasses and advice from gas-station attendants. In such instances, the gentleman must express abject humility, breathing deeply, swallowing hard, and admitting, "You're right, I should have stopped back at the last overpass. Any ideas as to what we should do now?" Once he and his date arrive at their destination, he must make all apologies and explanations, accepting all blame and allowing himself to be the brunt of all jokes.

WHEN A GENTLEMAN REALIZES THAT HE HAS, IN TRUTH, SAID SOMETHING THAT HAS HURT ANOTHER PERSON'S FEELINGS . . .

If he cares at all for the other person's feelings, he makes a straightforward apology, avoiding all temptation to make excuses for himself. The best apology is the simplest: "Jill, I'm afraid I hurt your feelings the other night. Please know I'm sorry. I didn't mean to offend you." It is never a gentleman's place to decide whether another person has any right to be offended. Even if he is convinced he was not in the wrong, at least he has done his best to stay on cordial terms with a person whose opinion he values. If the offended person continues to take umbrage, prolonging the pain by saying, "That was one of the ugliest things anybody's ever said to me. I've been telling everybody about it," the gentleman can only repeat his initial apology: "Again, let me say I'm sorry to have hurt your feelings." After that, he tries to change the subject, leaves the room, or considers whether he is perhaps wasting too much energy on this particular friendship.

WHEN A GENTLEMAN ARRIVES HOME AT TWO IN THE MORNING, WHEN HE'D PROMISED TO BE THERE FOR DINNER AT EIGHT—AND HE'S GOT LIQUOR ON HIS BREATH . . .

He is wise to avoid trying to explain his actions. A gentleman recognizes, right off, that two o'clock in the morning is no time to conduct a nuclear summit meeting, especially if he's had a few too many brewskies. Instead, except for frequently expressing remorse for his behavior, he shuts up and takes his knocks. If his loved one continues to press him for an explanation, he declines to offer one—at least at that moment—admitting the obvious facts that he's had too much to drink and that he'll be much better equipped to discuss his misbehavior—and accept his penance—after he's had a few hours of sleep.

Later in the day, he faces the offended party, frankly admits his error, and tells the truth about his whereabouts between eight and two the preceding evening. In no case does he put the blame on the faithful soul who has been left in the lurch. He never passes the buck by asking, "What's the matter? Don't you trust me?" or by attempting to avoid his responsibility with childish arguments such as, "Don't I have a right to my own friends?" or "Maybe if you'd stop nagging me, I'd get home on time."

At the earliest opportunity—that evening, or perhaps the next evening—if tempers have cooled, he attempts to set things right by arranging a nice dinner or sending flowers. It does no good for him to say, "It'll never happen again," unless he actually changes his behavior. If he finds he is having trouble getting control of his bad behavior, he may want to seek professional help.